TAROT
DECODER

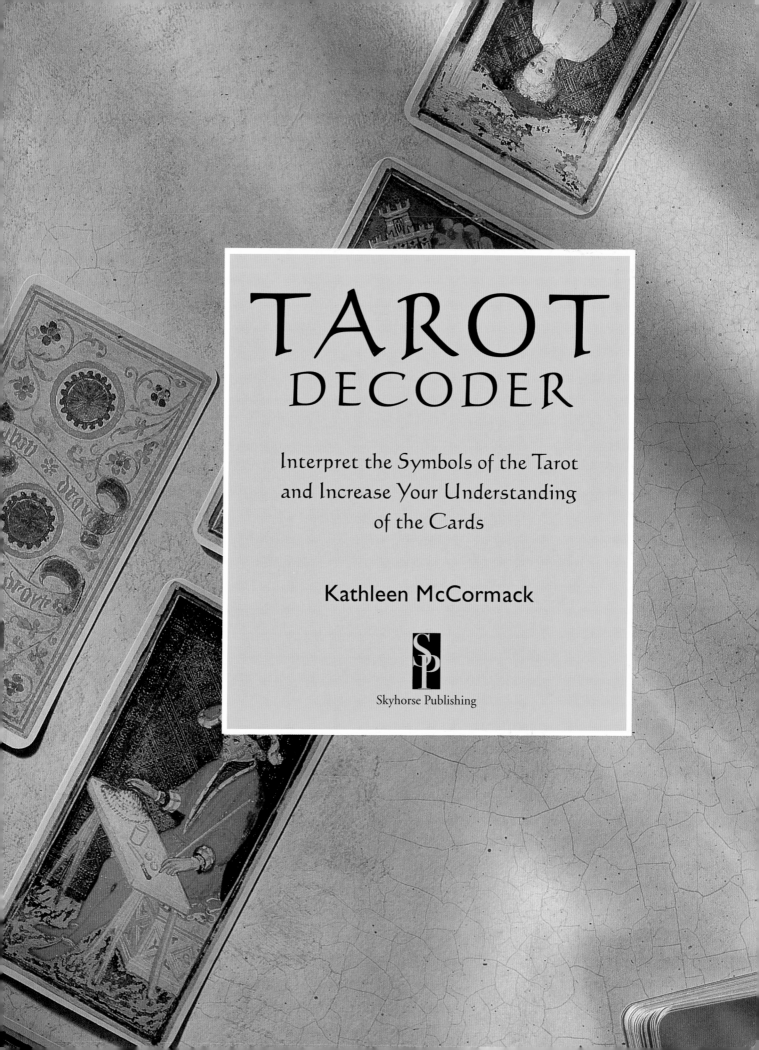

TAROT
DECODER

Interpret the Symbols of the Tarot
and Increase Your Understanding
of the Cards

Kathleen McCormack

Skyhorse Publishing

Copyright © 1998 Quarto Inc.

This edition printed 2014 by Skyhorse Publishing, Inc.

Skyhorse Publishing books may be purchased
in bulk at special discounts for sales promotion,
corporate gifts, fund-raising, or educational
purposes. Special editions can also be created to
specifications. For details, contact the
Special Sales Department, Skyhorse Publishing,
307 West 36th Street, 11th Floor, New York, NY
10018 or info@skyhorsepublishing.com.

Skyhorse® and Skyhorse Publishing®
are registered trademarks of
Skyhorse Publishing, Inc. ®,
a Delaware corporation.

This book produced by Quantum Publishing Ltd,
6 Blundell Street, London N7 9BH.

www.skyhorsepublishing.com

10 9 8 7 6 5 4 3 2 1

Library of Congress Cataloging-in-Publication Data
is available on file.

ISBN: 978-1-62873-667-0

Printed in China

CONTENTS

Introduction

Many people have intuitive experiences but only a few develop their psychic sense. Some ignore the experiences, because they are afraid, or believe them to be evil; others consider intuition irrational. Experiments to test for psychic abilities began in the 1930s at Duke University, North Carolina. These tests showed that there are people with the ability to see into the future, or into the past, and many of the individuals studied possessed a telepathic sense. The term E.S.P. (extra-sensory perception) was established to cover a range of psychic abilities, including telepathy, clairvoyance, recognition, and psychokinesis.

The Tarot has served scholars and seers for centuries as a stimulus to their intuitive powers and an aid to divining the future. Make the cards the focus of daily meditation by concentrating on their mythical symbolism and its hidden meanings. When you still the conscious mind in this way, you allow the supraconscious to come into play. This helps you to make the best use of your psychic ability. And the first person to look at is yourself. In order to grow spiritually, we need to love and accept ourselves. Only then can we genuinely accept and understand other people. The power of the Tarot carries with it the great responsibility of using the cards constructively, to find the right path in life, so always conduct readings with great sensitivity and care for others' feelings.

There are many different Tarot decks available to buy, and there is no right or wrong deck to use - it is really a matter of personal preference. It has never been easy to memorize the meanings of such a large number of cards, and because it is vital never to make up an interpretation, in the past psychics would often write the meanings on the cards. Nowadays many people type or write them on labels and paste them to the back of the cards I highly recommend this practice, particularly for those who are new to the Tarot.

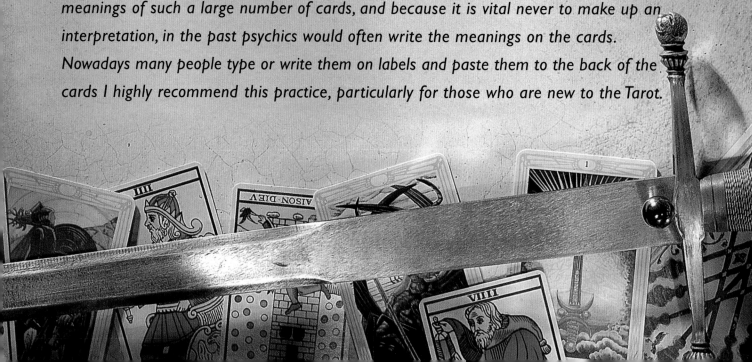

The History of The Tarot

The early history of the 78 Tarot cards is shrouded in mystery and speculation. Some believe that they derived from the sacred books of ancient Egypt. Others that they originated in India or China, and were brought to Europe by gypsies. Some think that they were invented by a group of medieval cabalists. Influences as varied as the Greek mystery religions, Gnosticism, Neoplatonism, Hermetism, Catharism, ancient Arabian and Indian philosophies, and the Jewish cabala have been detected in their symbols. The Tarot has been claimed to enshrine the secrets of the universe and to hold the key to the true nature of human beings.

Early Cards

The oldest description we have of a set of Tarot cards dates from 1392, when three decks were bought for King Charles VI of France. The cards, commissioned from an artist – thought to have been Jacques Gringonneur, who was also an astrologer and cabalist – were undoubtedly magnificent, as befitted their royal beneficiary. Seventeen cards, painted on vellum, with gold edgings and depicted in silver, lapiz lazuli, and a dark red pigment known as "mummy's dust," were long thought to belong to this set. They are now, however, judged to be Italian and of later manufacture.

Tarot cards almost certainly preceded playing cards designed for entertainment, to which they are related. Examples exist of 15th-century decks of cards used for games and also for education – a set depicting the order of the universe, for example. But records show that playing cards were widespread in Europe earlier than this. Gambling with cards was banned in what is now Germany as early as 1378, but in 1379 card-playing was one of the events at a festival in Brussels, and, in the same year, the ledgers of the Duke of Brabant (also in modern-day Belgium) recorded money paid for a set of cards. In the following year the Code of Nuremberg

Right: *The Tarot has been linked to medieval Italian pageants, known as Triumphs, and the earliest cards may have been gifts from the artists who worked on the pageants to their patrons. Such Triumphs may be the origin of our word "Trumps" for the major cards.*

Below and below left: *The High Priestess and the Cobbler from a 15th-century Italian deck made for the Milanese Visconti family. Their beautiful images are painted on vellum and edged with gold.*

permitted card-playing, and three years later it was sanctioned in Florence. But in 1397 people in Paris were still prohibited from playing cards on working days.

The imagery of the Tarot and other cards has been linked with the pageants held in Italian cities in medieval times. Called Triumphs, these were usually commissioned by one of the noble families and were dramatic stories with a moral theme, possibly related to the ancient mystery plays. Arranged in honor of a dynastic marriage or a visiting Church dignitary, or to celebrate a saint's day, the pageants developed into costly and complicated tableaux that eventually required the invention by engineers of mechanisms to animate them, and the designs of famous artists, such as Leonardo da Vinci, to stage them. A card game named Triumphs existed from the 14th century, and may have developed from cards commemorating one such pageant, commissioned by the patron or presented to him as a souvenir by the grateful artist.

The Burning of the Tarot

During the later Middle Ages many sets of Tarot cards were burned by the Church, which opposed gambling, with its emphasis on luck, and saw card-playing as a means of uniting people in sin. The first known attack on card-playing was written in 1377 by a Swiss monk. The target of his criticism seems to have been a deck not of 78 cards, nor even the 22 major cards of the Tarot, but a set of 56 cards – possibly the forerunner of our modern playing-card deck. In 1450, a Franciscan friar in northern Italy denunciated the pagan imagery on the picture cards. His attack on card-playing continued the theme of a crusade against the widespread Italian practice of gambling led by St Bernadine of Sienna. In 1423 Bernadine was responsible for the destruction of many decks of cards designed for the great Italian families. The Visconti deck, created for Filipo Visconti, Duke of Milan, was fortunately saved from the flames, and remains one of the most famous Tarot decks in existence today.

Printed Cards

Despite religious opposition, the use of cards, whether for diversion or divination, continued to flourish. The development of woodblock printing in Europe enabled card manufacture to become an industry, and men and women card-makers and painters were registered at Nuremberg. Leading artists continued to be commissioned to create individualized decks for wealthy clients. After seeing a deck of 98 Tarot cards in Florence, known as the Minchiate, at the end of the 15th century, the painter and engraver Albrecht Dürer returned to Germany and created a version of his own.

In 1463, the pragmatic English king Edward IV found it necessary to pass a decree, not to ban gambling, but to prohibit the importation of foreign cards. Card-making had become such a commercial success that English manufacturers were under pressure and there was a serious risk to the balance of trade.

Individualized Decks

Because of the number of surviving decks from Italy, some people locate the origins of the Tarot there. The deck designed in Bologna in 1412 by Frances Fibbia, the exiled Prince of Pisa, is claimed by some to be the originator of the 78-card deck that we know today, although it had no minor cards under six. Called the Tarocchino, the set was evidently intended for a game of the prince's own invention, and was highly praised in its time. It combined the minor, suitcards with an older deck of picture cards that may have been used for predicting the future, since even today some fortune-tellers withdraw all cards numbered below six from their decks.

Some people think that the prince either invented the Tarot symbols or adapted them from an older model. Certainly his 22 major cards seemed to symbolize the spiritual and moral struggle

Above: *An engraving of 12 cards from a 16th-century Minchiate deck. The deck features the signs of the zodiac, the four elements, and the four cardinal virtues, as well as the more usual Tarot images.*

of the human being's journey through life, and his sequence ended with Judgment.

The artist Marziona de Tartona copied the Bologna deck in 1415, adding the missing cards under six and bringing the total to 78. Another early Italian deck, the Florentine (or Minchiate) that inspired Dürer, comprised 78 Tarot cards, but added 12 astrological signs, the four elements – earth, air, fire, and water – and four of the seven virtues, Faith, Hope, Charity, and Prudence.

Over the centuries, as historians and occultists studied the Tarot, many created their own decks. These include the Wirth, the Grand Etteilla, the Thoth, and Rider decks. Some comprise variations of the old designs and names or symbols in keeping with the designer's interpretations. However, the designs used on the Marseilles deck that is generally accepted as standard today – and which are featured throughout this book – are based on medieval sources, researched by the French historian Antoine Court de Gébelin in 1773, and many are scarcely altered from the original woodcuts.

Below and left: *The Ten of Pentacles and Ace of Swords from a 15th-century Italian deck designed for the Visconti family. These cards are among the most famous Tarot cards in existence.*

The Minor Arcana

The 56 minor cards, or minor arcana, are divided into four suits, each containing cards numbered from ace to ten and four court cards, originally known as "coat cards." These are the queen, king, knight, and a young person who was originally of either sex, entitled knave, page, or maid of honor. Knave originally meant son, so the court cards are believed either to depict a well-to-do medieval family, or a royal couple with token defender and servant.

The four suits – Swords, Pentacles, Wands, and Cups – were traditionally linked with the ancient astrological symbols of the lion, the bull, the eagle, and the angel (or man), which became the four animals of the Apocalypse in the vision of the Old Testament prophet Ezekiel. Medieval artists equated them with the four cardinal elements – fire, earth, air, and water – and with the four seasons – summer, spring, fall, and winter. These were associated, in turn, with the Hebrew letters IHVH, or Jehovah (seen as the conscious energy from which the universe was created). The four suits were also thought to derive from the four sacred objects of the Grail legends: the sword, dish, lance, and cup. Others believe they derived from the four classes in society, with Cups representing the Church, Pentacles representing money-makers, Swords the fighters, and Wands the farmers. There is also the view that Cups could have represented the aristocratic class, Wands the landowners, Pentacles the tradesmen, and Swords the fighting men.

In the 15th century a French knight, Etienne de Vignoles, adapted the minor arcana to create the game of piquet. Our modern pack, which is derived from his, has Hearts in place of Cups, which gives the suit the connotation of love and happiness; Diamonds in place of Pentacles, derived, it is believed, from the diamond-shaped tile, or "carrefour," on the floor of the Money Exchange in Paris because of the suit's association with money; Clubs in place of Wands, the club's shape derived from the trefoil or clover, meaning fertility and creative work; and Spades in place of Swords (*espada* is the Spanish word for sword), which derived either from the piques or lance points, or the handle of a sword, and carries the meaning of strength, conflict, and spiritual struggle.

Asian Origins

The rich symbolism of the cards exercises a continuing fascination, hinting at powerful, hidden, and possibly impenetrable mysteries. The 56 minor cards seem relatively familiar: four suits that appear to correspond roughly with our Hearts, Diamonds, Clubs, and Spades. It is the 22 major cards, or major arcana, however, that excite most speculation. And because no one knows the origins of the Tarot for certain, theories abound.

A 15th-century Italian writer named Covelluzo claimed that the cards had entered Italy from Arabia, brought by Arab merchants. Certainly, the Italian and Venetian ports were bustling centers of commerce in the Middle Ages. Travelers such as Marco Polo, who visited China, India, and other parts of Asia in the 13th and early 14th centuries, had opened up new worlds. Sea traders brought in the philosophies of the East along with their exotic cargoes. They are said to have introduced circular playing cards from China, which were later adapted in Venice to become the Tarot's minor arcana. Some modern scholars believe that four ancient cards in the Bibliothèque Nationale in Paris are of Venetian origin, and were the models of all other Tarot decks.

Some detect a link between the major arcana and the metaphysical teachings of India, notably Buddhism, the religion and philosophy founded more than 500 years before Christ by Siddhartha Gautama (the Buddha, or "Enlightened One"). The Chariot is thought to represent the Juggernaut or triumphal car; the Wheel of Fortune to be the Wheel of Rebirth; and the Devil to depict Yama, the god of death. The other cards of the major arcana are said to be elements of Buddha's life and experiences before his enlightenment. Certainly the Tarot deals with similar concepts, expressed in accordance with Western tradition.

Codes for the Initiated

The idea of the Tarot as a coded system of preserving important knowledge has led some to link it with the great library at

Left and below: *Some scholars have linked the symbolism of the major arcana with that of Buddhism, with the Devil representing the god of death, the Chariot the triumphal car, and the Wheel of Fortune the Wheel of Rebirth. The cards shown here are from the IJJ Swiss deck.*

Alexandria in Egypt, founded in the 4th century BC. When the library was destroyed some 700 years later, they claim, the city of Fez in Morocco became the intellectual center of the ancient world. Scholars came to confer from so many countries that an easily understood form of communication was needed. A book of mystic symbols was invented, and its key taught orally. Later, to ensure that the knowledge would not be lost, yet would remain accessible only to the initiated, the symbols were reproduced on playing cards, used also by those who remained ignorant of their message.

The Knights Templars

Another, more widely supported theory holds that the cards were invented by the Knights Templars, an ascetic and military order of knights formed from among the Crusaders in about 1118, under the leadership of Hugh de Payen. Their mission was to protect pilgrims and guard the routes to the Holy Land. In time, the order became so powerful and wealthy that it was perceived as a threat by King Philip IV of France. In 1307 he confiscated its property, and charged the Knights with heresy on the basis of what many now believe to have been false testimony. The Templars were accused of worshiping an idol known as Baphomet, and having statues in their meeting places which were considered by the Church to represent the devil. The figures were depictions of Mithras, a Persian god, whose worship spread to ancient Rome and was popular throughout the Roman Empire, because of its promise of human redemption and eternal life. Mithras was associated with the sun and with astrology, and his ritual involved secret initiation ceremonies in underground temples. Many of the Knights Templars, including their leader, were tortured into confessions – publicly renounced later in the case of the leader – and were burned at the stake.

The Knights Templars were officially disbanded in 1312, but groups survived, and the mystique that had surrounded the Order for 200 years continued to intrigue people down the centuries. To this day, individuals and organizations claim to be the inheritors of the Templars' secrets and their rites. The Knights did indulge in mysterious practices; symbolic carvings in

their meeting places suggest that they may have engaged in alchemy, mystic geometry, numerology, and astrology (identical with astronomy at the time). By virtue of their military role in the Near East, they were exposed to unfamiliar ideas derived from Islamic and Judaic culture. They were influenced also by their Cathar recruits, who espoused the beliefs of Gnosticism – a system that combined mythology, ancient Greek philosophy, ancient religions, and Christianity, that viewed matter as evil and emphasized a personal union with the divine. Whether the Templars worshiped idols, or merely adorned their meeting places with emblems considered appropriate for a military order, we do not know. However, symbols linked to them can be found in many Tarot

Below: *Crusaders such as the Knights Templars (right) were renowned for their secret rituals. Their symbology can be found in many Tarot decks.*

Left: *This painting depicts a group of young people playing a game with Tarot cards. Despite centuries of opposition from the Church, card-playing remained a popular past-time. Cards from the suit of Wands and the suit of Pentacles can clearly be seen. The four suits of the minor arcana are the forerunner of the suits of our modern deck – Wands became Clubs, Pentacles became Diamonds, Cups became Hearts, and Swords became Spades.*

decks, and the picture of the Devil in 18th-century decks – perhaps inspired by a contemporary revival of interest in the order – is consistent with the Mithraic statues associated with the Templars.

"Know Thyself"

Many myths that surround the Tarot seem to emanate from the time of the Renaissance, when a new spirit of learning was abroad in Europe. From the mid-14th century onward, scholars became increasingly interested in the works of classical Greek and Roman authors, and began to rediscover classical ideas. The development of the printing press made classical, religious, scientific, and philosophical texts, along with other information and opinions, available to a greater public than ever previously possible, and disseminated ideas that challenged the prevailing orthodoxy.

To some of the questing minds of the Renaissance, the Greek gods and goddesses, with their differing spheres of influence, their human as well as godlike attributes, and the sometimes darker side of their natures, seemed a more appropriate symbolic representation of the complex universe and the laws of creation than the religious precepts of the day. Above the door of Apollo's temple in Delphi stood the words "Know Thyself," but this was an alien concept to a Christian Church that believed in strict obedience to its teachings and for which the greatest study of mankind was not man. Renaissance scholars were inspired by the the ideas of Platonic and Hermetic philosophers, who stressed the importance of personal development, and the artists and sculptors of the time began to portray classical gods and goddesses in addition to conventional religious figures.

Tarot in the Monasteries

Nevertheless, and in spite of the Church's opposition to the evils of cards, it may have been monasticism that helped to preserve the Tarot. Medieval monks favored a system of memory training known as a mnemonics, which used a series of pictorial images as an aid to recollection. (The Stations of the Cross in Catholic churches, which are a focus for meditation on the events leading to the death of Jesus, can be seen as a modern continuation of this.) One such medieval memory system is the Baldini deck of cards previously attributed to the Italian artist and engraver Andrea Mantegna but now thought to date from slightly earlier. The deck, featuring 50 pagan images, is believed to have been used by the Pope and his cardinals during their seven-month ecclesiastical council in 1459 to relieve their boredom. Preserved in the monastery libraries were old grimoires (books of magic spells) concerning alchemy and astrology, and the sacred books of persecuted sects, such as the Gnostics and the Albigensians, showing the classical gods in various guises, which were studied by the monks as examples of Satan's many manifestations.

Memory, Meditation, and Magic

The Tarot cards are said by some to be coded symbols drawn from a Gnostic or Albigensian book of learning. Alternatively, it has been suggested that the mnemonic system, which originated in ancient Greece (the name comes from the Greek for "mindful"), involved meditation upon a series of images with a higher meaning, symbolizing the divine law of the universe. The purpose of the meditation was to attain a level of spiritual consciousness where the soul was enriched by the power of the divine. The monks were not alone in their use of mnemonics. With Renaissance interest in the ancients, talismans, magic emblems, and classical images became associated with memory systems, and it is possible that the major arcana derived from one of these.

The fact that the major arcana number 22 has led some to discern a cabalistic source for the Tarot, because in cabalistic numerology, 22 is the number of "all things": the entire universe. The cabala was a collection of Jewish mystical tradition and knowledge concerning the nature of the universe. Its ultimate origins are obscure, although some aspects of it may derive from ancient Egypt, but it first came to prominence in 12th- and 13th-century France and Spain, and was eagerly taken up by Christian humanists during the Renaissance. Esoteric and abstruse, it has a number of ideas in common with Gnosticism, but was traditionally perceived as having links with magic. This was regarded by early cabalists as a dangerous corruption of the cabala, but was exploited by later occultists, who added their own interpretations to the original writings.

The cabalistic importance of the number 22 is linked to the 22 letters in the Hebrew alphabet and the 22 paths on the Tree of Life, which link all the aspects of the divine that underlie the universe and the nature of human beings. The Tree is a configuration of the emanation of the universe from God, representing the descent of the divine into the human and the road by which the human can ascend to union with the divine. The number and symbolism of the major arcana and the formation in which they are laid out could reflect this view of the construction of the universe.

Below: *The mysterious emblems and potent symbols of witches and sorcerers have been compared to those of the Tarot, a link exploited by many occultists through the centuries.*

The Wisdom of Ancient Egypt

The view of the Tarot as a compendium of ancient mystical wisdom was adopted with particular enthusiasm in 18th-century France. This was the "Age of Enlightenment," prior to the French Revolution, when humanitarian ideals were burgeoning and dogma was once again being challenged. Secret and semi-secret societies were founded, which looked to the Templars as earlier exemplars of the anti-clerical ideas that were in the air. Freemasons of the day claimed for themselves the inheritance of the Templars' rituals and their arcane secrets.

In 1773 the French scholar and freemason Antoine Court de Gébelin wrote a series of books entitled *Le Monde Primitif,* which discussed the customs, science, and religion of the ancient world and compared them with the civilization of his day. In volume 8, he examined the Tarot and pronounced it to be of ancient Egyptian origin. He asserted that the Tarot was a remnant of the sacred book of the Egyptian god Thoth, patron of scribes and magicians, whose functions included weighing the human heart during the judgment after death. The Greeks and Romans associated Thoth with their messenger god Hermes/Mercury. They regarded him as the founder of alchemy, in which mercury, the element named for the god, is accorded great power. Thoth acquired the title Hermes Trismegistus (the Thrice-Great Hermes) from the Neoplatonists, who named alchemy "the hermetic art" in his honor. According to legend, 42 hermetic books were written at the dictation of Hermes Trismegistus, setting out the philosophy of ancient Egypt. It was de Gébelin's belief that the surviving fragments, in the form of the Tarot, had been preserved by the Gypsies following their exodus from ancient Egypt.

When he first encountered the Tarot, de Gébelin realized that the cards were of considerable antiquity, and he noted that although they had been used for centuries in Belgium, Italy, Germany, and Spain, for gambling and for divination, they were little known in France outside the south of the country and the port of Marseilles in particular. This was an area inhabited by large numbers of Gypsies. The Gypsies, who reached France in the 15th century, were initially thought to have come from Egypt (the name Gypsy derives from "Egyptian"), although they originated from India, and migrated through Persia to Europe.

Below: *Egyptian artifacts brought to Europe by Napoleon in the 18th century excited the popular imagination, and the Tarot was widely believed to have originated in ancient Egypt.*

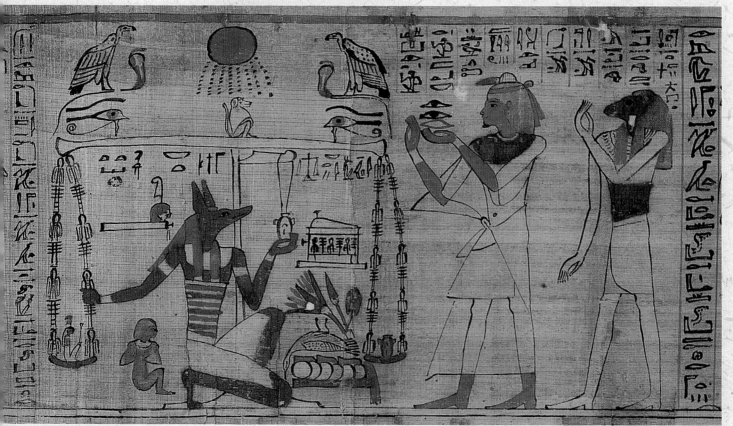

De Gebelin's ideas were enthusiastically taken up by a Parisian barber named Alliette, who rose to fame as a fortune-teller under the pseudonym Etteilla (his name spelled backward). His book on the Tarot, published in 1775, and a deck of his own devising, were notable more on account of his showmanship and financial flair than for the authenticity of his research. He stressed the divinatory aspect of the cards, and their links with astrology and the cabala, but his alterations and interpretations were denigrated by scholars and subsequently disregarded. Etteilla was not the only French fortune-teller to turn to print. One of his most famous successors was Marie Le Normand, whose reputation was assured when she predicted Napoleon's marriage to Josephine. She developed her own methods, and her book on cartomancy and her own set of cards, based loosely on the Tarot, are still available.

Toward the end of the 18th century, de Gebelin's theory gained impetus from the interest surrounding Napoleon's expedition to Egypt. The arrival in France of tablets, statues, papyri, and other antiquities, bearing their mysterious hieroglyphics, prompted a fascination with everything Egyptian. Excitement was succeeded by disappointment for some, however, when the Rosetta stone, discovered in 1799, which provided the key to ancient Egyptian writing, failed to reveal any links with the Tarot.

Early 19th-century scholars, such as Jean Duchesne (writing in 1844) and William Chatto (writing in 1848), dismissed the Egyptian theory as too far-fetched, and declared the Tarot to be European, and Samuel Singer, writing in 1816, had preferred the 15th-century finding of Covelluzo, that the cards had originated in Arabia.

Above: *Gypsies have long been associated with divination and Tarot cards. The Romany word for a deck of cards is Tar, giving credence to the view that Gypsies brought the Tarot to Europe.*

The Gypsy Connection

The association of the Tarot with the Gypsies was less readily discarded, however. The French scholars Boiteau d'Ambley, who wrote a treatise on playing cards in 1844, and J. A. Vaillant, who wrote a treatise on the Gypsies (or Romanies, as they are also known, from their native name *Rom*) in 1857, both claimed that the Tarot belonged to the Romanies. D'Ambley wrote that the slight oriental influence he detected in the cards derived from the era when the Gypsies fled from India to Persia before coming to Europe. Vaillant had lived with the Gypsies and based his opinion on an expert knowledge of their language (Romani), culture, and history.

This theory was rejected by fellow Frenchman Romain Merlin, writing in 1869, on the grounds that the Tarot had been known in Europe long before the recorded arrival of the Romanies at Lüneburg, Germany, in 1417. However, there is evidence that Gypsies were wandering in Europe considerably earlier than that. Like de Gèbelin, the writer Paul Huson, one of the finest modern authorities on the origins of the Tarot, noted their presence in southern France, and renewed speculation about links between those Gypsies and Egypt. He pointed out that the shrine of St. Sara, the patron saint of the Gypsies, at Les Saintes Maries de la Mer in the Camargue region of southern France, lies on the legendary site of an ancient altar to Mithras. The pantheon of Mithras had assimilated the Egyptian god of the dead, who was renamed Sarapis.

According to another modern writer, Wenzell Brown, the Gypsies have always claimed to possess a secret book of great antiquity, which is the true guide to divination by the cards. Their methods of divination are apparently handed down orally from mother to daughter, however, and no copy of the alleged book has ever been discovered. A more convincing association lies in the Romany language, which derives from a pure form of Sanskrit, the oldest of the Indo-European languages. The Romany word for a deck of cards is *Tar*, from the Sanskrit *Taru*.

In 1855, Alphonse Louis Constant, a famous French occultist and prolific writer on magic, under the pseudonym Eliphas Lévi, placed his weight behind the theory that the Tarot came from an ancient civilization in the Middle East and was carried to Europe by the Romanies. Lévi, who had trained for the priesthood and professed himself a Catholic all his life, evolved a new interpretation of the Tarot based on the cabala. This was a period of enormous interest in the occult, and Lévi's writings in the domain were highly influential. His ideas continued to shape attitudes toward the Tarot until at least the 1920s, and a deck based on his ideas, designed by Oswald Wirth, exists today.

The Rosicrucians

Lévi's writings inspired a group of occultists, magicians, and Symbolist poets to found a movement based on the ideas of the Rosicrucians – an early 17th-century order dedicated to the pursuit of knowledge and mystical speculation. During the 18th century, Rosicrucianism had become entangled with freemasonry, and had acquired considerable emphasis on esoteric symbolism and ritual. The 19th-century Rosicrucians included Papus (Gérard Encausse), a doctor of medicine who founded a school of the occult in the 1890s. In 1889 he published *The Tarot of the Bohemians*, setting out his belief that the major arcana symbolized the spiritual journey of mankind. He incorporated Lévi's theories and Wirth's cards, allied the minor arcana with the Hebrew system of numbers, and introduced interpretations of these cards through sets of three: beginning, highest point, and decline.

Correlations with the cabala and the 22 paths of the Tree of Life also informed the teachings of The Hermetic Order of the Golden

Below: *The mystery that enshrines the Tarot's origins has fascinated scholars and diviners for centuries, many of whom have created their own Tarot decks, such as the Thoth deck shown here.*

Dawn, an English magical society, established in 1887–88, many of whose members were Rosicrucians. One of the order's founders was a scholar of repute, Samuel MacGregor Mathers, who defined the Tarot as "a treatise on human will and spiritual enlightenment." He altered and expanded the ideas of Lévi, changing the numerical sequence of the major arcana and incorporating astrology into the interpretations. Another member of the order, the notorious devotee of the occult Aleister Crowley, reinterpreted the symbolism of the Tarot and designed his own deck, known as the Thoth deck. He believed that the Fool should begin the major arcana sequence and be numbered 0, and most modern decks follow his thinking.

A New Deck

In 1916, the American occultist and writer Arthur Edward Waite, also a Golden Dawn member, worked with artist Pamela Colman Smith on the design of a new Tarot deck. Known as the Rider-Waite deck – Rider comes from the name of its London publisher – it departed from tradition by incorporating Rosicrucian concepts into a number of the major arcana and, more strikingly, recreating the minor arcana to show scenes instead of a pattern of symbols. Although Waite and Smith received much criticism from occultists and scholars for their amendments to age-old principles, and for the unattractiveness of the new deck, their interpretations made the Tarot much more accessible to those who found other decks difficult to understand, and the Rider deck is one of the most widely used today.

Enduring Power

Explanations of the history and meaning of the Tarot continue to be suggested. Whatever its origins, however, there was almost certainly never a single way of interpreting the cards. So evocative is their symbolism that no two people are likely to draw exactly the same associations from them. The mystery of the Tarot may lie beyond words, and the wisdom we can draw from it may be only as much as we need to aid our own perceptions. There is no doubt, however, that the cards embody an aura of mystery and a power that should never be misused.

Reading
The Cards

Learning the meanings of the Tarot cards is like learning the rules of English. Until you know them, you cannot write in an individual style. Having learned the conventional meaning, you might find that a certain card speaks to you in another way. So be it. We all see the world differently, and if the message you glean from the card is in tune with your psyche, who can say you are wrong? At first you may find it helpful to write the meanings on labels and paste these to the back of cards.

Preparing for a Reading

If you have psychic ability, concentrating on the cards can give you insights into future or past events. If your intuition is as yet undeveloped, practice will help it to grow and strengthen. An awareness of the spiritual dimension of life, plus a trust in the intuitional faculty, can lead to the development of a psychic sense, which will be peculiarly the property of each reader. You will eventually be able to give the cards distinctly individual interpretations, but before this stage is reached, the traditional meanings must be learned and card-reading practiced to enable intuition, inner awareness, and sensitivity to others to develop.

1. The person who reads the cards is known as the reader. and the person they are reading for is the querent. It is the custom to wrap the Tarot cards in a black cloth, preferably silk, which is thought to protect them from both negative and positive vibrations. Most readers allow no one to touch their cards, which they believe to possess their personal aura.

2. Many readers turn a third of cards upside-down to invert them before shuffling. Most readers shuffle the deck themselves, and ask the querent only to cut the deck. This must be done with the left hand — once believed to be the hand ruled by the devil and by the physical or conscious mind, but later seen as representing the spiritual and the subconscious.

Asking a Question

Although it has long been customary for the querent to ask a specific question, people often prefer not to divulge personal information especially if they are skeptical of the reader's psychic ability Sometimes querents ask about an unimportant issue, because they are afraid to express, or even to confront, what is really worrying them. In spite of this, the intuitive reader can usually offer the advice needed to solve the real problem.

Readers who know that they possess strong telepathic powers and are concerned that they could tune directly into the querent's mind, rather than their own supraconscious, often insist on using a second deck of cards. This is both shuffled and set out by the querent to check that the psychic evaluation is the same.

Right: *If negative cards appear in a spread, always try to interpret them kindly and search for the positive aspects. The positive major arcana card Strength, for example, always supersedes any negative cards. The card shown here is from the Ukiyoe deck.*

3. *The querent cuts the deck into three, placing each pile face down in a row from left to right.*

4. *When turned face up, the top three cards are generally considered to give an overview of the answer to the querent's question. The reader then picks up the three piles, from right to left, and holds them face down in the palm of the left hand, ready to layout the first spread.*

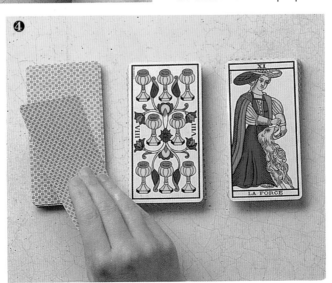

Relaxation and Empathy

To begin a reading it is important to relax the mind, so that it is open to the messages the Tarot symbols will send you. When you have decided which spread (layout) to use (see pages 24–27), and are ready to set out the cards, spend a few moments meditating or praying for guidance. You can also protect yourself by visualizing a shining gold ring encircling your body and then closing up around your chest. Some psychics do this to safeguard themselves against an encounter with people of a strongly combative or negative nature that can drain their energy. If you sense a loving positiveness in your querent, however, visualize building a golden bridge between that person and yourself.

Remember that in every reading, no matter what negative messages the cards bring, you must always try to put yourself in the querent's place and interpret them in the kindest way possible.

21

Choosing a Significator

In several of the methods of setting out the cards, such as the Celtic Cross spread used throughout this book, your first task is to select a card to represent the querent. This card is known as the Significator. If the querent's question is of an emotional or spiritual nature, it is traditional to choose a card from the major arcana, the Pope for a male or the High Priestess for a female. If the question concerns material matters, however, the Significator is usually a court card from one of the suits of the minor arcana. Many readers prefer to use court cards whatever the question.

In addition to their individual meanings, the court cards denote a person's age, sex, and coloring, as illustrated to the right. Your querent may not fall neatly into a single category, so you will have to use your own judgment to choose the card you feel most closely represents him or her. Older people are generally represented by Pentacles or Cups when their hair goes gray. As you become more intuitive, you may prefer to choose a Significator that represents the querent's inner qualities rather than outward appearance. In addition, although the cards are portrayed as male or female, the attributes they represent can apply to either sex. Because maturity varies with the individual and is not necessarily linked to chronological age, an experienced reader might sense that the querent is older or younger than the representative card suggests, and has qualities associated with a court card of a different sex than their own. Use the following as a guide:

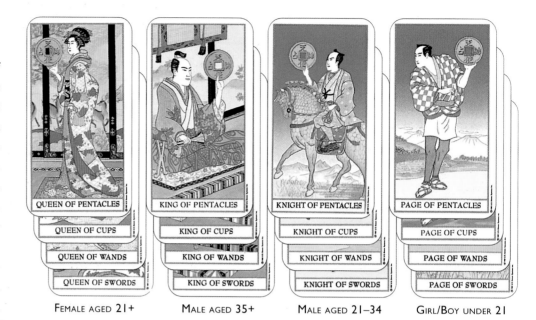

FEMALE AGED 21+   MALE AGED 35+   MALE AGED 21–34   GIRL/BOY UNDER 21

Pentacles: *Blue or gray eyes; light blond or red hair; fair or freckled skin.*

Cups: *Blue eyes; dark blond or light brown hair; medium-to-fair skin.*

Wands: *Hazel, brown, or green eyes; brown hair; olive skin.*

Swords: *Dark brown or black eyes; black hair; dark skin.*

- **The king embodies a positive, experienced, intelligent, sometimes aggressive and dictatorial, outgoing force.**
- **The queen characterizes an intuitive, sympathetic, nurturing, and occasionally manipulative, inner power.**
- **The Knight symbolizes a youthful, energetic, pioneering, passionate, rash, and sometimes selfish personality.**
- **The Knave represents qualities of spiritual emergence, an artistic or intellectual flowering, or the beginning of something that needs protection in order to develop.**

Areas of Meaning

Always analyze a larger spread before carrying out a smaller, more specific reading, in order to obtain an overall view of the querent's future prospects. Study all the cards in the spread. If a number of the major arcana appear, it will denote that the events they portray will be of lasting importance to the querent. It could also signify that the querent has a strong and courageous nature and definite views on life. See if you feel there are too few or too many of the major arcana cards present. Too many can indicate a strongly controlled person, who cannot express his or her true feelings and may be near to breaking point. Too few can denote deep inner distress, because the querent is not facing his or her problems squarely.

The meanings of the major arcana will overshadow those of the minor, but the minor will add more clarity to the foreseen events and give more depth to the spiritual and emotional problems the querent may encounter. The four suits of the minor arcana represent the four elements, and the preponderance of any minor suit in a spread means that the area it rules should be paramount in the reading. The primary areas ruled by each suit are as follows:

- **Wands symbolize fire, life, growth, and work of all kinds.**
- **Cups denote water, emotions of love and pleasure, the subconscious, fertility, and beauty.**
- **Pentacles represent the Earth, the five senses, money, magic, and trade.**
- **Swords stand for spiritual struggle, physical conflict, courage in the face of enmity, and strength in adversity.**

If the querent has a specific problem, choose one of the smaller spreads, using only the relevant suit of the minor arcana:

- **For career matters, use Wands.**
- **For emotional matters, use Cups.**
- **For spiritual conflict or decision, use Swords.**
- **For money matters, use Pentacles.**

If the problem concerns deep spiritual issues or choices, the major arcana should be used instead.

If there is a preponderance of court cards in any spread, it indicates that many people are involved in the situation, although sometimes a court card can mean an event rather than a person, and occasionally both. The inner qualities of the court cards may mirror the querent's own inner nature, or the card may depict a person with those qualities who will act as a catalyst to teach the querent more about themselves and so assist in their self-development. Sometimes a court card will turn up in a spread representing the querent as either older or younger than he or she actually is, possibly because that person is either perpetually young at heart or perhaps preternaturally bowed down by worry or hedged around by tradition and convention.

Modifying Factors

Reversed cards deal with character development and the inner psyche. Many Tarot readers do not favor reversals, declaring that they were only introduced in the mid-19th century, possibly by Etteilla, the French barber-turned-clairvoyant, who may have introduced the practice in order to make reading more difficult for the lay person. Whether this is true or not, it is a fact that some readers prefer not to use reversals, believing there are sufficient unfavorable meanings in the upright cards to give an accurate reading. However, some of the suit cards have predominantly negative meanings when upright, and if reversed are more positive, and many readers feel it is beneficial to take these into account.

Right and below: *It is easy to see if a picture cord is reversed, but you may find it useful to mark the top or bottom of the deck for the lower suit cards, as reversals are less obvious.*

The Spreads

There are many methods of setting out Tarot cards for a reading. Dealing repeated small spreads is preferable to setting out all of the 78 cards, and missing the meaning because the pattern is too complicated. The spreads on these pages are some of the most effective and widely used. The larger spreads are suitable for a general view of the querent's life, the smaller spreads for a more specific reading.

THE SIMPLE DRAW

1	2	3

This is an old Romany method used to answer a specific question. Ask the querent to draw three cards at random from the deck. The first card indicates the past, the second the present, and the third the future. If no clear answer appears, repeat the process a second and third time. The summing up of the nine cards should then give the solution.

THE HEXAGRAM SPREAD

A reading used to answer a specific question, the hexagram spread uses six cards plus the Significator, which is placed in the center. Deal the cards clockwise, beginning at the top. The top triangle of three cards – numbers 1, 2, and 6 – is linked and reads as positive. The cards of the inverted triangle – numbers 3, 4, and 5 – are the influences working against the querent.

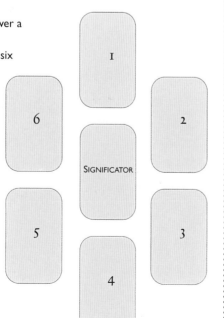

THE MAJOR ARCANA QUICK SPREAD

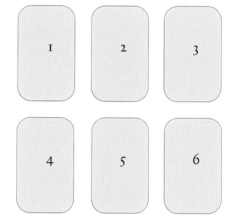

Use this spread only for serious issues or for the answer to a vital question.

Method

1 Shuffle the major arcana, and ask the querent to cut them into three piles, face down and from left to right.

2 Turn the three piles face up, remove the first three cards, and place them in a row, from left to right.

3 Repeat the procedure, so that you have two rows of three cards in front of you.

Interpretations

The center cards in both rows – number 2 and number 5 – are the important cards in this spread. They determine the final outcome, or give the answer to the problem. The top line – numbers 1, 2, and 3 – tell of events which will happen in the near future. The bottom line – numbers 4, 5, and 6 – tell of events which will happen at a later time. Cards 5 and 6 denote the unexpected happening, or an obstacle, and cards 1 and 4 denote benefit and helpful influences.

THE CELTIC CROSS

The Celtic Cross, which is shown in detail throughout this book, incorporates cards taken from the entire deck and is usually used to answer a specific question. Select a Significator that is suitable to the questioner and the question. Place the Significator face up on the table. Concentrate on the question, shuffle the deck, and ask the querent to cut the cards into three piles, face down and from left to right, using the left hand. Some readers look at the three top cards to gain a preliminary idea of the outcome. Others simply pick up the three piles, from right to left, hold them face down in the left palm, and begin to layout the spread.

Diagram

| 5 Possible goal or outcome | | 10 The final outcome |

| 4 Past influences | I / 2 Immediate influences / Present position of querent | 6 Future influences | 9 Querent's hopes and ideals |

| | 3 Recent influences | 8 Family and friends |

| | | 7 Querent's negative feelings |

Method

I Place the first card on top of the Significator.

2 Lay the second card across the first.

3 Place the third beneath the Significator.

4 Put the fourth card on the left, behind the Significator.

5 Lay the fifth card above the Significator.

6 Put the sixth on the right, in front of the Significator. You have now formed the cross.

7 Build a vertical line to the right of the cross with the four remaining cards, starting from the bottom with the seventh card.

Interpretations

If there is a majority of major arcana cards in the spread, powerful influences are at work in the querent's life, or are influencing his or her unconscious mind. This suggests that destiny may take a hand, and put the result out of the querent's control.

When a court card of any suit covers the Significator in the first position of the Celtic Cross, firstly read all the cards and assess the complete situation before deciding whether this card could represent a person other than the querent, or the querent, or if an alternative meaning should be chosen.

If a court card appears in the tenth position, the outcome may be decided by a person of that age and coloring. Remember that although there are ten positions in the Celtic Cross, each with individual meanings, the cards are linked and the interpretation of the tenth card should include all that has been divined from the other cards in the spread.

If the outcome is inconclusive, lay another Celtic Cross on top of the first, using the tenth card as Signficator.

There are 10 positions in the Celtic Cross spread. They represent:

I What covers the querent: the present situation that surrounds the question

2 What crosses the querent: the influences or obstacles connected with the question

3 What is beneath the querent: recent past influences that have affected the question

4 What is behind the querent: the past events that form the basis of the question

5 What crowns the querent: the possible goal or outcome of the querent's present position

6 What is before the querent: immediate future influences connected with the question

7 Negative emotions: the fears of the querent

8 Family and friends: present opinions of the querent's family and friends

9 Positive emotions: hopes and ideals of the querent

10 The outcome: the final result, or answer to the querent's question

THE 21-CARD SPREAD

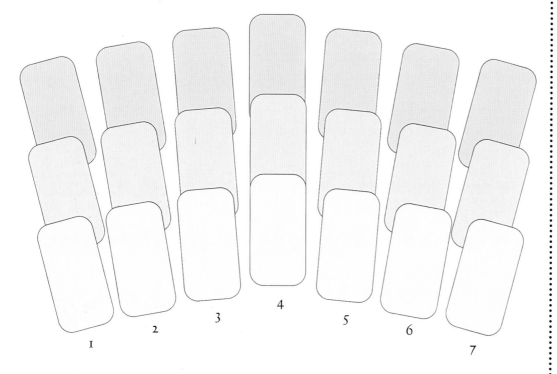

This is a traditional spread to answer a specific question. Choose an appropriate Significator to represent the querent, but do not take it out of the deck. Shuffle the deck in the usual way before laying out the cards.

Method

1 After shuffling the deck, fan out the cards face down on the table.

2 Ask the querent to pick 21 cards at random.

3 Deal the 21 cards from left to right in seven piles of three cards.

The seven piles denote:

1 Events that will occur in the querent's home life

2 Events pertaining directly to the querent

3 Influences from the querent to his or her friends, or vice versa

4 Whether the querent's wish will be granted

5 What is not expected but may eventuate·

6 What is expected and may not eventuate

7 What is sure to come true

Interpretations

If the card you would have picked to represent the querent as the Significator appears in any of the seven piles, it indicates that the final outcome could be altered by the querent's attitude or a decision that he or she makes.

Often the cards in positions 1 and 2 refer to the same thing, or to two events which will follow each other.

The cards in positions 5 and 6 refer to the main situation which was revealed in the preceding piles. Sometimes the cards in positions 3 and 5 only refer to peripheral events in the querent's life.

If the Nine of Cups is present in position 4, the querent's wish will be granted. An even more fortunate and powerful result will occur if a benevolent major arcana card, such as the World, Star, Empress, or Sun, or the strongest and most stable of the minor arcana, the Nine of Clubs, appears in this position.

The cards in position 7 summarize the reading and present the answer to the querent's question.

THE 42-CARD SPREAD

This is an ancient method said to have been favored by Italian "witches," and used in Europe from the Middle Ages. Its thorough mixing of the cards accentuates the element of fate, and it lacks the specific areas of interpretation that appear in the Celtic Cross and some of the smaller spreads. It therefore provides less guidance to the reader, so it is recommended for the more intuitive person who is completely familiar with the meanings of the cards.

Method

1 Shuffle the deck in the usual manner, place the cards on the table, and invite the querent to select 42 cards at random. Ask the querent to place the first six cards face upward in a line, from right to left. Repeat this process, laying each subsequent row of cards on top of the previous one, until there are six piles, each consisting of seven cards.

2 Pick up the first heap of seven cards on the right (the reader, not the querent), and set them out face up in a row, this time from left to right. Pick up the second heap of cards on the right, and deal these on top of the first row, but this time from right to left. Repeat this process with all six piles of cards, alternating the direction in which they are laid out, until there are seven piles of six cards each.

3 Take the top card from each of the seven heaps, shuffle them, and set them out from right to left in a new line

26

4 Remove the next two top cards from each heap, shuffle them, and place them in two lines under the first seven cards, again from right to left.

5 Finally, shuffle the remaining 21 cards and lay them in three lines beneath the others, in the same way. You should now be looking at six rows of seven cards, laid out row upon row.

Interpretations

In this spread, the Hierophant represents a male querent, and the High Priestess a female. If the spread contains either or both of these cards, some readers take them out and place the Hierophant on the right for a male, and the High Priestess on the left for a female, and use them to influence the overall reading.

Because the major arcana can give strength to a reading, however, some people prefer to leave these two major cards in the spread, and choose the applicable court card to place alongside instead. If you do choose to remove them, ask the querent to draw another card from the remaining 36 cards of the deck to fill the vacant space on the table.

Begin your reading by concentrating on the symbology of the cards, which will trigger your memory and your intuitive powers. Remembering that each card also influences the card next to it, link them together into a story. Start slowly at the top right-hand corner and work across the rows, zigzagging from right to left, then left to right, until you reach the bottom right-hand corner.

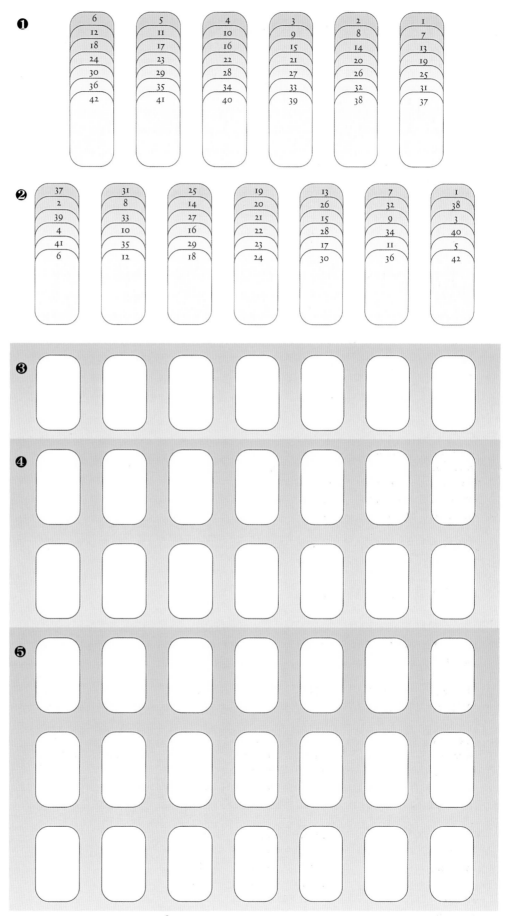

❶

6	5	4	3	2	I
12	II	10	9	8	7
18	17	16	15	14	13
24	23	22	21	20	19
30	29	28	27	26	25
36	35	34	33	32	31
42	41	40	39	38	37

❷

37	31	25	19	13	7	I
2	8	14	20	26	32	38
39	33	27	21	15	9	3
4	10	16	22	28	34	40
41	35	29	23	17	11	5
6	12	18	24	30	36	42

❸

❹

❺

THE PYRAMID SPREAD

This spread is used to answer a specific question. It involves laying out an upright pyramid of cards, followed by an inverted pyramid. First, shuffle the deck in the usual way.

Method

I Deal the first eight cards face down in a row, from right to left. Deal the next six cards, again from right to left, and position them centrally above the first row. Continue until you have built a pyramid of 21 cards in fives rows Turn over cards 7, 14, and 21 to obtain an overview of the spread. Then turn over all the cards and interpret them for a general view of the querent's current situation.

| 21 |
20	19
18	17	16	15
14	13	12	11	10	9
8	7	6	5	4	3	2	1

Interpretations

The first part of the spread, the upright pyramid, gives an overview of the querent's situation. The bottom row of cards in this pyramid represent the past influences that relate to the situation. Card 21 is the most important card, and represents the influences that are now dominant. This card affects the whole reading.

The inverted pyramid gives a more specific answer to the question being asked. It should be interpreted in relation to the overview given by the upright pyramid.

2 Pick up the 21 cards of the upright pyramid, and shuffle and cut them. Put them back with the rest of the deck, and shuffle and cut the whole deck once again. Deal out the first card face upward. Place the second card to the left of it. Use the next three cards to create the tip of an inverted pyramid. Deal out the next two cards to complete the base of the pyramid. Use the inverted pyramid spread to give the answer to the question.

| 2 | 1 | 7 | 6 |
| 3 | 5 |
| 4 |

The seven cards in the inverted pyramid denote:

I Past influences

2 Present influences

3 Future influences

4 What the querent should do about the situation

5 The attitude of those around the querent

6 Obstacles

7 The final outcome

THE CIRCULAR SPREAD

This spread is used to give a general forecast for the year ahead. It is unusual in that both the reader and the querent shuffle the deck.

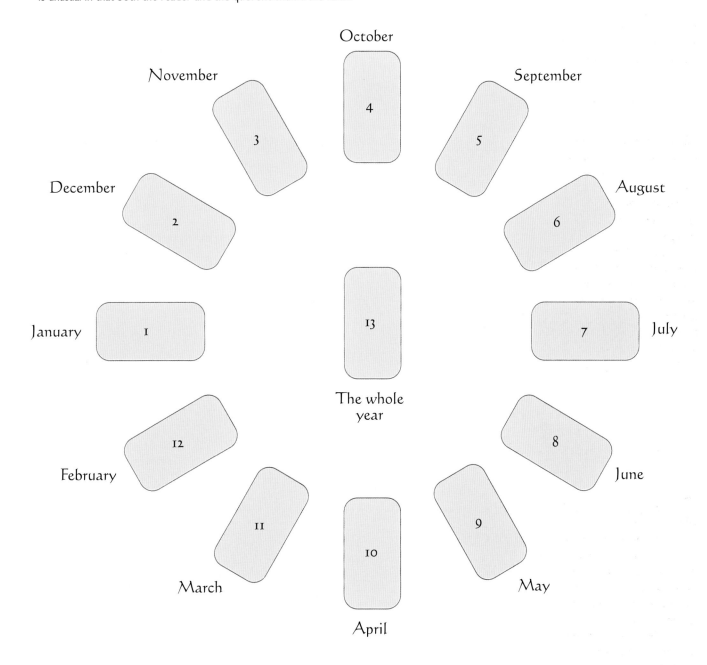

October

November

September

December

August

January

July

13

The whole year

February

June

March

May

April

Method

1 The reader should shuffle the deck first, followed by the querent. The reader then deals the cards. Place the first card face upward on the left-hand side, in a position corresponding to 9 o'clock on a clock face.

2 Deal the next 11 cards in a clockwise direction, placing each one face upward in a circle, with each card corresponding to one of the positions on a clock face.

3 Once the circle is complete, place the 13th card in the center.

Interpretations

Start the interpretation with card 13 in the center of the circle. This card gives an overview of the year ahead, from the time of the reading. Each card represents a month in the coming year. Read the cards in a counterclockwise direction, starting with the card that corresponds to the month in which the reading takes place. All cards should be interpreted with their upright meanings, whether they are upright or reversed. Always keep card 13 in mind when interpreting the cards for each individual month.

The

Major Arcana

The major arcana consists of twenty-two picture cards, numbered one to twenty-one. The Fool is usually unnumbered, although some decks label it zero. The cards, also known as "Trumps," are rich with ancient symbolism, and dominate the reading of a spread. This section decodes the symbols and describes the meanings most often ascribed to the major arcane, to inspire your own specific and relevant interpretations. Cards from the traditional Marseilles deck, whose images have inspired most modern decks, are depicted throughout and their symbolism explained. The Thoth deck, with its innovatory designs, is also pictured, to demonstrate the continuing evolution of the Tarot and its symbolism.

The Fool

The Fool, or Jester, is one of the most significant cards in the Tarot, representingt he seeker of experiences. It can imply the beginning of a new chapter, possibly with a risk involved that requires wisdom and courage. It can also mean recklessness and lack of motivation if reversed.

SUGGESTED READING

1 Upright or Reversed Fool
Pure-minded with a childlike faith in miracles. The querent is independent, rebellious, adventurous, and loves life.

2 Upright or Reversed Fool
A brand new chapter in life is about to begin

3 Upright Fool
Independence of thought and originality are the basis of success.
Reversed Fool
Irresponsibility and rebellion can be destrμctive if they are taken to extremes

4 Upright Fool
Great potential results from seeing and doing things in a revolutionary way..
Reversed Fool
Recklessness with money can cause hardship.

5 Upright Fool
Travel in hope and reach eventual fulfillment.
Reversed Fool
When reaching crossroads, think carefully about future direction in life.

6 Upright Fool
Success comes from being adventurous and trying new methods.
Reversed Fool
Indiscretion and trusting in the wrong people could spoil everything.

7 Upright Fool
Listen to own inner voice, not to others.
Reversed Fool
Learn from past mistakes. Look before you leap.

8 Upright Fool
Maintain equilibrium; neither good nor bad luck is permanent.
Reversed Fool
Don't brood about injustice. Discuss troubles openly.

9 Upright Fool
If the voice of the heart is heard, a new life will begin.
Reversed Fool
Excitement and travel beckon.

10 Upright Fool
A significant leap in spiritual advancement brings lasting inner peace.
Reversed Fool
An important decision needs careful thought to ensure future happiness.

---

5 Possible goal or destiny

10 The final outcome

1

2 Immediate influences

Present position of querent

4 Past influences

6 Future influences

9 Querent's hopes and ideals

8 Family and friends

3 Recent Influences

7 Querent's negative feelings

Combinations of Cards

This card combines only with those cards which are highly spiritual, and is canceled out by powerful material cards, such as the Wheel or the Devil. If it follows the Hermit, a secret will come to light. If the Hermit comes after it, a secret is now safe. The Fool with the Chariot denotes important news. The Fool and the Sun mean something unexpected will bring order, comfort, and happiness.

The Fool is the eternal traveler, ready to set forth alone in search of life's secrets.

LE · MAT

B·P·GRIMAUD·PARIS 1981

His cap is sometimes depicted as horned, and is thought to derive from the horns or ears of an ass worn by the rebellious Dionysus during the winter festival of misrule.

The combination of the cults of Mithras (god of light) and Dionysus (god of wine) produced rites and feasts such as the winter festival of the rebellious Lord of Misrule, or Dionysus in revolt, who symbolized the search for spiritual enlightenment and rebirth. The Fool, in the motley clothes of a court jester, is his descendant.

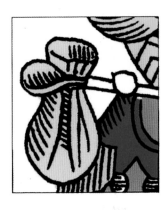

He carries a small bundle, tied to the end of a stick, across his shoulders. Early moralists thought it contained all the worldly sins and vices.

He is portrayed striding out carelessly across the countryside with a staff in his hand and a dog snapping at the bag hanging from his belt. He must make his choices, abandon, adopt, embrace, or discard, in order to attain perfection.

Wearing spring green, the April Fool bursts forth to seek new experiences.

The Cobbler

This card is depicted as either a Cobbler or Magician, and represents self awareness, skill with the written or spoken word, a love of new ideas, and a willingness to take risks. It also implies guidance by occult forces, and when reversed can mean trickery and misuse of occult powers.

SUGGESTED READING

I **Upright or Reversed Cobbler**
The commencement of some creative project, turning thoughts into positive action.

2 **Upright or Reversed Cobbler**
A sudden beneficial change of career, a new direction in life, or an important breakthrough in consciousness.

3 **Upright Cobbler**
A readiness to be daring to achieve success.
Reversed Cobbler
A warning that methods used to gain objectives may not be entirely ethical.

4 **Upright Cobbler**
A recently started undertaking has brought satisfaction and happiness.
Reversed Cobbler
A chance for a new beginning ignored, or the querent may be seeking the wrong goal.

5 **Upright Cobbler**
Something novel and exciting which brings triumph through courageous action.
Reversed Cobbler
Delayed success through lack of confidence..

6 **Upright Cobbler**
Something that will alter the future, or the strong support of a loving friend.
Reversed Cobbler
Must see both sides of the matter to be successful.

7 **Upright Cobbler**
A positive approach ensures success.
Reversed Cobbler
Time will be lost through worrying about risks.

8 **Upright Cobbler**
Your knowledge will impress others and they will approve of your plans.
Reversed Cobbler
Make sure you have all the correct facts and that you are acting with the right motives.

9 **Upright Cobbler**
Spiritual and psychic powers to be used for others.
Reversed Cobbler
Care is needed to avoid misusing psychic power or manipulating others.

IO **Upright Cobbler**
A triumphant new beginning. A creative success.
Reversed Cobbler
Success will come later through self-awareness.

Card positions

5 Possible goal or destiny	IO The final outcome
I	9 Querent's hopes and ideals
2 Immediate influences	
4 Past influences	6 Future influences
Present position of querent	8 Family and friends
3 Recent Influences	7 Querent's negative feelings

Combinations of Cards

If the Cobbler and Death are opposite each other in the fifth and tenth positions, the result will be a cancellation of an event. If they appear next to each other anywhere, they cancel each other out. If the Cobbler is opposite either the Devil or the Wheel in the fifth or tenth position, a delay will occur. If the Cobbler is reversed in front of the High Priestess, it denotes occult power wrongly used.

With his vivid attire and symbolic tools; the Cobbler is a master of his craft.

The Cobbler wears multicolored garments and a large brimmed hat, shaped like a figure eight, which is said to represent the cosmic lemniscate, the ancient Egyptian symbol of eternal life.

LE · BATELEUR

Some decks show a plain girdle, but others emphasize the duality of this card by depicting a girdle shaped as a snake holding its tail in its mouth. This symbolizes eternal truth, knowledge, and duality, the union of the personal and the divine, power, subtlety, and diplomacy. On the negative level, it symbolizes the use and abuse of occult power, domination, deceit, trickery, and lies.

His left hand holds a small rod or tool, possibly derived from the caduceus, the traditional wand of the messenger god Hermes/Mercury

Various tools of the Cobbler's trade lie on the bench in front of him, including the four suit emblems. The cup represents emotions and sex, the sword or knife willpower and intellect, the pentacle symbolizes the financial and physical aspects of life, and the rod or wand spirituality.

The Magician; or Magus; juggles symbols of the four elements; the written word; willpower; and wisdom.

The Magus

The High Priestess

A card of deep mystery and duality, the High Priestess can denote inner perception, strong artistic and creative abilities, a thirst for learning, and a desire for independence. When reversed, it can imply undeveloped talents, fear of commitment, hypocrisy, and problems in physical and emotional relationships.

5 — Possible goal or destiny	10 — The final outcome
1 — Immediate influences	9 — Querent's hopes and ideals
2 — Present position of querent	
4 — Past influences	6 — Future influences
	8 — Family and friends
3 — Recent Influences	7 — Querent's negative feelings

SUGGESTED READING

1 Upright or Reversed Priestess
Independent, intuitive, and perceptive, with a deeply spiritual soul. Too generous and open, sometimes with a strong creative urge.

2 Upright or Reversed Priestess
Creative talents demand expression, or a spiritual person will influence and encourage the querent to use artistic or psychic abilities

3 Upright Priestess
New phase of life beginning. Desire for self-development and possible occult experience.
Reversed Priestess
The querent must learn to be self in all situations and have faith in own abilities.

4 Upright Priestess
Support lacking through giving to wrong people.
Reversed Priestess
Living superficially; jealousy and hostility toward others.

5 Upright Priestess
Success in using talents to encourage and uplift others.
Reversed Priestess
Have faith in own judgment.

6 Upright Priestess
Self-motivation and self-discipline will bring rewards.
Reversed Priestess
Learn to be a graceful receiver, and allow others to show their feelings to you.

7 Upright Priestess
Listen closely to own feelings and intuition.
Reversed Priestess
Keep intentions and confidences to self; others are not as trustworthy as yourself.

8 Upright Priestess
Fear of commitment could delay happiness.
Reversed Priestess
Independence of mind and individuality can sometimes spoil relationship with others.

9 Upright Priestess
Inner commitment and artistic achievement.
Reversed Priestess
Lack of support could bring an end to a relationship.

10 Upright Priestess
Success and lasting contentment will occur.
Reversed Priestess
Entire picture cannot be seen; await developments. There will be eventual success.

Combinations of Cards

If placed next to the Wheel. and both cards are upright, it means recompense in a lawsuit or petition which seemed hopeless at the outset. When reversed, it means loss of stability and possibly violent upheaval. If reversed and followed by an upright Temperance, it indicates that prospects are very dark, since this combination brings bewilderment and difficulty in finding a solution.

With her miter and book, the High Priestess suggests authority with understanding.

The High Priestess was early associated with Juno, in her dual aspect as queen of heaven, protectress of women, and queen of the dead. Juno was, in turn, identified with the Egyptian goddess Isis and with Diana, goddess of the moon. But from medieval times, the Priestess was depicted in ecclesiastical robes, and accorded the title La Papessa.

Crowned with the papal miter, the High Priestess owed her status to the 13th-century legend of the female Pope Joan, said to have been born in Germany of English parents, and to have been elected pope in 855 under the name John VIII. But some see Joan as a manifestation of Juno, and the canopy behind her head could be an echo of the horned headdress of Isis, representing the crescent moon.

The book in her lap is a symbol of esoteric wisdom and law, of spiritual knowledge and teaching, and of oracular ability. Some decks show her with a partly unrolled scroll, bearing the letters TORA, which is believed to represent the Torah, or divine law.

Bathed in a veil of light, the Priestess possesses inner perception and knowledge.

THE MAJOR ARCANA

The Empress

This is a card of abundance – in natural, emotional, and material resources. It often stands for renewal and nurture: a birth, a creative endeavor, a return to health after illness. It can mean wealth, reward for effort, and warm family life. But its reverse is extravagance, laziness, maternal tyranny, destruction, and waste.

SUGGESTED READING

5 Possible goal or destiny

10 The final outcome

1 Immediate influences

2 Present position of querent

9 Querent's hopes and ideals

4 Past influences

6 Future influences

8 Family and friends

3 Recent influences

7 Querent's negative feelings

1 **Upright or Reversed Empress**
Hard-working individual with protective instincts; father or mother figure, intuitive rather than logical, emotional, loves comfort, attracts wealth.

2 **Upright or Reversed Empress**
A new beginning, demanding patience and skillful nurturing.

3 **Upright Empress**
A partnership, business, or artistic venture, which is bound to be successful.
Reversed Empress
Be practical and take responsibility on own shoulders or venture will fail.

4 **Upright Empress**
Endurance, determination, and thrift used in past to achieve, and must be used again.
Reversed Empress
Prospects could be blighted through extravagance.

5 **Upright Empress**
Great benefit accrues from seeds sown in past.
Reversed Empress
Responsibilities toward self and loved ones could cloud attitude to others in society.

6 **Upright Empress**
Economic success, emotional or physical healing, reconciliation after separation.
Reversed Empress
Impractical dreaming could stop plans being actualized.

7 **Upright Empress**
Strong intuition must be used to connect with own spiritual nature.
Reversed Empress
Be careful. Know what is needed, not what is wanted.

8 **Upright Empress**
A friend or partner will need encouragement.
Reversed Empress
Failure to allow others freedom to develop brings emotional instability.

9 **Upright Empress**
Recognition, financial expansion, and reward.
Reversed Empress
Good counsel and financial advice are needed to prevent failure.

10 **Upright Empress**
Eventual gain much larger than anticipated.
Reversed Empress
Inevitable benefit, though slightly delayed.

Combinations of Cards

When this card precedes the Cobbler, diplomacy brings success. If the Empress precedes the Chariot, there will be a decisive victory in material matters. If the Empress is reversed in the same position, the victory will be delayed but inevitable. When the Empress is reversed and followed by a strong card, such as the Devil, the Tower, or Death, they cancel each other out.

38

The Empress is lovely, and possesses all the trappings of luxury and material power

L'IMPÉRATRICE

Her shield depicts a golden eagle, a representation of courage and power, borne by the Romans on their standards and scepters. The golden eagle was adopted by the knights of the Crusades, and in mythology it was linked with the sun. It has been the royal or imperial emblem of many nations and a religious symbol identified with preaching.

The Empress holds the scepter, which has been a symbol of imperial might since ancient times, and is traditionally bound with gold. It derived from the wand, and in Greek legend the scepter of the gods held miraculous powers. The ball, or orb, is also an emblem of empire, and is surmounted by a cross to signify the rule of spiritual over temporal power.

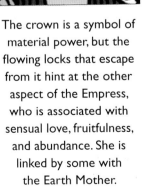

The crown is a symbol of material power, but the flowing locks that escape from it hint at the other aspect of the Empress, who is associated with sensual love, fruitfulness, and abundance. She is linked by some with the Earth Mother.

The Empress holds an open lotus flower, representing femininity and natural abundance.

The Empress

The Emperor

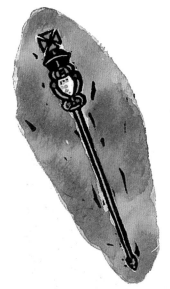

The Emperor is a card of leadership, often at a high level. It represents stable government, worldly wealth and power, authority, self–discipline, and the rule of law. There is passion, but intellect dominates intuition. Reversed, it indicates egocentricity, a need to dominate, fixed opinions, immaturity, and an obsession with fame and fortune.

5 Possible goal or destiny	**10** The final outcome
1 **2** Immediate influences Present position of querent	**9** Querent's hopes and ideals
4 Past influences	**6** Future influences
	8 Family and friends
3 Recent influences	**7** Querent's negative feelings

Combinations of Cards

When the Emperor precedes the World, and is upright, it means a lull in war, a state of truce, or a transient peace. If reversed, the card can mean conflict, or loss of power or position in the world. When the Emperor is surrounded by cards from the suit of Pentacles, it denotes the offer of an authoritative position concerned with high finance, which carries onerous duties or heavy responsibilities.

SUGGESTED READING

1 Upright or Reversed Emperor
A leader with gravity, authority, and dignity who is parental in attitude.

2 Upright or Reversed Emperor
Government, officialdom, or authoritative older professional or businessman will advise or help.

3 Upright Emperor
Actualizing ideas with the help of powerful man or perhaps the government.
Reversed Emperor
Be careful always to finish one project before embarking on another one.

4 Upright Emperor
Rectifying matter with aid from established source. Sometimes concerned with armed forces or government.
Reversed Emperor
Too strict control; needless intervention stifles initiative.

5 Upright Emperor
Success and high position; founding a new business with official help.
Reversed Emperor
Need discipline and control to maintain balance and prosper.

6 Upright Emperor
Using own initiative, taking responsibility.
Reversed Emperor
Obsession with power is a dangerous thing.

7 Upright Emperor
Keep sense of adventure; courage and kindness will stand you in good stead.
Reversed Emperor
Being dogmatic can stifle inner development.

8 Upright Emperor
People who depend too much on the strong can become a burden.
Reversed Emperor
Unnatural constraints can inhibit development.

9 Upright Emperor
A born organizer and successful achiever.
Reversed Emperor
A leader must learn to discipline self before others.

10 Upright Emperor
High office, leadership success, or big business opportunity.
Reversed Emperor
Delayed outcome through ruthless competition or government regulations.

The Emperor is the counterpart of the Empress, but depicts force and dominance.

The Emperor is viewed from the side, only half sitting on his throne, mentally alert and poised for action, despite his apparently relaxed stance, which is also in the form a symbolic cross. One foot is firmly planted on the ground; mountains, representing terrestrial domination and unyielding power, are pictured in the distance.

The beard is an ancient symbol of wisdom and endurance, the qualities of a great leader. The Emperor's crown is reminiscent of a military helmet, linking him with Mars, the god of war.

The Emperor's shield is set imposingly beside his throne, rather than held for protection. The eagle, with wings outstretched, stands astride the land in a posture of dominance.

The Emperor brandishes the upright scepter in a gesture of might over the outside world. The cross is an ancient symbol that predates Christianity. The Emperor's cross could be related to the crux ansata, the ancient Egyptian symbol of eternal life.

The pillars of the Emperor's throne have ram's heads as their capitals, representing dominating force.

The Hierophant

Also known as the Pope, this card indicates conventional adherence to established forms of religion, and a desire to conform and gain social approval. It can imply a scientific, philosophical, educational, or religious vocation, or inspiration in the performing arts. A reversed card can denote delayed ambitions, hippie tendencies, or innovation.

5 Possible goal or destiny			**10** The final outcome
1 / **2** Immediate influences Present position of querent			**9** Querent's hopes and ideals
4 Past influences		**6** Future influences	**8** Family and friends
3 Recent influences			**7** Querent's negative feelings

SUGGESTED READING

1 Upright or Reversed Hierophant
The querent seeks for true meaning to life. Has philosophical, religious inclinations, and teaching and counseling ability.

2 Upright or Reversed Hierophant
New opportunity for work or study.

3 Upright Hierophant
Delayed ambition or a late vocation.
Reversed Hierophant
There are many ways to free oneself from unhappiness.

4 Upright Hierophant
Experience is the best teacher. Learn from it.
Reversed Hierophant
Do not be hidebound. Explore new ways of thinking or working.

5 Upright Hierophant
An opportunity for career advancement. or a breakthrough in consciousness that destroys spiritual arrogance.
Reversed Hierophant
The heart rules and brings happiness to others through unselfish help.

6 Upright Hierophant
There must be solid organization before success can be achieved.
Reversed Hierophant
Be aware that outward appearance can sometimes become too important.

7 Upright Hierophant
Do not be influenced by others. Have faith in oneself.
Reversed Hierophant
An nonconformist. open to new ideas.

8 Upright Hierophant
Remember that everyone can be wrong sometimes, not just others.
Reversed Hierophant
Avoid giving overemphasis to innovation and change

9 Upright Hierophant
Self-fulfillment, success, a position that serves society.
Reversed Hierophant
Take care that facts are not distorted to fit beliefs.

10 Upright Hierophant
Success through selfish action brings acclaim but small reward.
Reversed Hierophant
Success will only come with courage of convictions.

Combinations of Cards

When the Emperor and the Hierophant come together it means a struggle between materialistic and spiritual desires. The outcome depends upon which card comes first. If both are reversed, and the Hierophant precedes the Emperor, wealth will be lost through pride, and failure in some enterprise is possible. If the other way around, wealth and power will be lost through lack of learning.

The Hierophant is shown as a spiritual and religious father, blessing and inspiring his flock

LE · PAPE

Although he wears a pontiff's crown, the Pope's other name derives from ancient Greece, where a hierophant was a priest of a mystery cult. He is seated between two pillars, representing Mercy and Severity, which some see as a link with Jupiter, the all-forgiving father, who controlled human affairs.

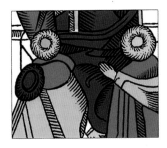

Tonsured priests kneel before him to receive his blessing, acknowledging his authority and wisdom, and his role in awakening inspiration in others.

The triple cross is a symbol of the papacy, but the glove bears the Maltese cross, the emblem of the medieval Knights of Malta. A religious military society, they were also known as the Hospitalers, because of their role in caring for the sick during the Crusades.

He lifts his right hand in benediction. In contrast with the High Priestess, or Papessa, who denotes esoteric knowledge, the Hierophant stands for the handing down of established teachings, control over the externals of religion, and spiritual domination. Nevertheless, some decks depict him holding crossed keys, an emblem of the papacy but also of hidden doctrine.

The Hierophant is seated on a bull representing strength and balance; the child at his heart symbolizes goodness.

The Hierophant

The Lovers

Trial and choice are the themes of this card. It suggests a decision based on intuition rather than intellect, choice between idealistic love and physical attraction, or love and career, but can also mean harmony and friendship. Its reverse can imply vacillation, infidelity, quarrels, and interference from others.

SUGGESTED READING

I Upright or Reversed Lovers
Querent finds choice difficult. Indecisive because of fears of hurting others.

2 Upright or Reversed Lovers
Choice to be made which tests values, with vitally important outcome.

3 Upright Lovers
Becoming conscious of self, and learning greater self-control through relationships with others.
Reversed Lovers
Another's point of view is equally valid.

4 Upright Lovers
An emotional trial which will be resolved successfully in time.
Reversed Lovers
Overdependence on others can often result in making the wrong choice.

5 Upright Lovers
True love or friendship based on equality.
Reversed Lovers
Beware of being dominated by the physical.

6 Upright Lovers
Opposites are two sides of the same coin; one cannot exist without the other.
Reversed Lovers
Inability to cope with uncertainty in relationships.

7 Upright Lovers
Choose intuitively and firmly, and victory is yours.
Reversed Lovers
Love triangle could eventuate unless honest with self.

8 Upright Lovers
Decision between love and career or domestic life and creative work.
Reversed Lovers
Negative influence of others could destroy relationship.

9 Upright Lovers
A flash of insight suddenly solves problem.
Reversed Lovers
Need for creating close bonds with others.

IO Upright Lovers
The right choice has been made after learning to accept self and others.
Reversed Lovers
Look carefully and choose path with care. Make sure it is what is really wanted.

Spread positions

5 — Possible goal or destiny

IO — The final outcome

I — (Immediate influences)

2 — Immediate influences / Present position of querent

4 — Past influences

6 — Future influences

9 — Querent's hopes and ideals

8 — Family and friends

3 — Recent influences

7 — Querent's negative feelings

Combinations of Cards

If the Lovers comes before the Chariot, there will be a betrayal. If the Chariot comes first, a sudden departure will end a venture or romance. The Lovers before the Cobbler means indecision in commencing a new venture, and the Lovers reversed in front of the Cobbler denotes a separation due to hesitation. If the Lovers is followed by cards from the suit of Swords, a relationship will end.

Victims of Cupid's bow express the eternal dilemma of choice, especially in affairs of the heart.

A young man must choose between two women of different ages and contrasting appearance. The scene derives from the Greek legend of the judgment of Paris, in which Paris had to choose between three goddesses, although the two women on this card could personify vice and virtue.

The oldest decks portrayed Paris with the three goddesses, offering a golden apple (the apple of discord) to the goddess of his choice. The other two deities did not forgive Paris's rejection. When he abandoned his wife for Helen of Troy, they are said to have caused the fall of Troy out of spite.

Eros, or Cupid, the god of love, appears as a winged boy, looking on in amusement at the young man's predicament, which was probably provoked by the god himself. Other decks portray Cupid as an angel, offering guidance to a young woman as she is beseeched by a lover.

Eros carries a bow and arrow for the purpose of piercing not the lover's heart but his or her eye, through which love was thought to enter the heart. The meddling Eros is reputed to have blinded Paris while he sought to make his judgment. Eros is said to carry a golden arrow for virtuous love and a leaden arrow for sensual passion.

The Lovers are opposites, one holding a wand (work) and the other a cup (emotion), to symbolize choices and dilemmas.

The Chariot

This card has implications of struggle and triumph against the odds. It can denote prestige and wealth through sustained effort. It also indicates unexpected news by word of mouth, and fast, luxurious travel. If reversed, it is a warning to control physical passions, vanity, and ruthlessness, and suggests the collapse of plans.

5 Possible goal or destiny	**10** The final outcome
1 Immediate influences / **2** Present position of querent	**9** Querent's hopes and ideals
4 Past influences	**6** Future influences
	8 Family and friends
3 Recent influences	**7** Querent's negative feelings

Combinations of Cards

Followed by the Moon, this card means that a secret will come to light. If the Chariot follows the Moon, there will be scandal or sickness, but if the Moon is reversed, this outcome will be less strong. If the Chariot precedes the Tower, it denotes that sustained effort will bring success; if before the Hierophant, it means success in a creative field; if before the World, ambitions will be fulfilled.

SUGGESTED READING

1 Upright or Reversed Chariot
Querent faces triumphant new beginning, but must learn to control emotions.

2 Upright or Reversed Chariot
Good news or spoken message brings change for the better.

3 Upright Chariot
Protecting own interests and inner psyche is a test which strengthens character and brings victory.
Reversed Chariot
Competition from others causes recognition of own aggression and ability to control own emotions.

4 Upright Chariot
Unexpected and exciting new start.
Reversed Chariot
Apply energy wisely and plan carefully, otherwise lack of direction could bring failure.

5 Upright Chariot
Great artistic success or triumph in work.
Reversed Chariot
Introspection and meditation are necessary to clear vision and reach goal.

6 Upright Chariot
Sustained effort will bring the beginnings of future progress and success.
Reversed Chariot
Over-emphasis on the physical side of life results in a loss of spirituality.

7 Upright Chariot
Peace after strife; triumph over ill-health.
Reversed Chariot
Wastefulness and self-indulgence can ruin prospects.

8 Upright Chariot
Opposition conquered, enemies routed.
Reversed Chariot
Unfortunate news brings plans to a head.

9 Upright Chariot
Wealth and honors will be achieved in time.
Reversed Chariot
Possible loss of partners or friends through arrogance and aggressive attitude.

10 Upright Chariot
Honor, recognition, or speedy, luxurious travel.
Reversed Chariot
Care must be taken that desire for success does not cause others to suffer.

A prestigious royal figure parades in his canopied chariot after a hard-won victory.

The two horses drawing the chariot are believed to represent emotion, which needs to be controlled In some decks, they are depicted as lions, resembling a talisman featuring a canopied chariot drawn by lions worn in ancient times to give a man courage and honor in war and success in competitive activities. In other decks they appear as a black and a white sphinx.

LE CHARIOT

The origin of this card is Ares/Mars, the son of Zeus/Jupiter, symbolizing divine destruction, making it the opposite of the Hierophant, who stands for divine stability. Mars was portrayed by many medieval artists, standing in a chariot, sometimes drawn by winged horses, and brandishing a whip or sword – here replaced by a scepter to denote triumph. The four pillars upholding the chariot's canopy are said to symbolize the cardinal elements: fire, air, earth, and water.

His military-style epaulettes suggest his role as the god of war, but they consist of two faces, thought to represent his rule over the opposing forces of emotion and intellect, or the carnal and the spiritual.

The chariot is pulled by four sphinxes and bears a triumphant figure, heavily armored after battle.

The Chariot

Justice

As its name implies, this card suggests fairness, honesty, the acceptance of responsibility, and a well-balanced outlook. It can indicate a just outcome, especially of legal or educational concerns, and the vindication of truth. Its reverse denotes indecision, difficult adjustments, over-harsh judgment, and bigotry.

SUGGESTED READING

1 Upright or Reversed Justice
Querent faces a matter that has to be weighed carefully before making a decision. Fight for what is right.

2 Upright or Reversed Justice
Person who will act as arbitrator in a matter, or give good advice to do with legal regulations or education.

3 Upright Justice
Balanced emotions result in harmonious partnerships.
Reversed Justice
Past legal matter which affects, present, or accepting consequence of own actions.

4 Upright Justice
Setting confused life in order. A well-balanced mind helps to bring a well-balanced environment.
Reversed Justice
Frustration and resentment through inability to adjust to circumstances.

5 Upright Justice
Legal victory or fair and just outcome of matter.
Reversed Justice
Delay occurs through various legal complications.

6 Upright Justice
Vindication of querent's moral character. Querent has integrity and balance.
Reversed Justice
Achievement is only possible through education.

7 Upright Justice
Look beneath the surface; do not judge others by appearance alone.
Reversed Justice
Do not judge others too harshly when all the facts are not known.

8 Upright Justice
Repayment of a debt in a gratifying way.
Reversed Justice
Try to forget past wrongs; events cannot be altered.

9 Upright Justice
Justice will be done and truth revealed.
Reversed Justice
Weigh every situation carefully and impartially.

10 Upright Justice
Victory and justice. An educated, powerful person will help outcome.
Reversed Justice
Victory will be achieved after mercy has been employed.

Card layout positions:

- 5 — Possible goal or destiny
- 10 — The final outcome
- 1 — (top)
- 2 — Immediate influences / Present position of querent
- 4 — Past influences
- 6 — Future influences
- 9 — Querent's hopes and ideals
- 8 — Family and friends
- 3 — Recent influences
- 7 — Querent's negative feelings

Combinations of Cards

If this card precedes the High Priestess, secrets connected with the law will come to light. If the High Priestess comes first, the meaning is the same, but the facts will only be revealed through legal affairs. If both are reversed, an event connected with the law or justice will miscarry. When Justice precedes the Hanged Man, tolerance should be shown rather than cold, hard judgment.

Grave and majestic, Justice bears the implacable sword and the balanced scales of judgment.

Justice was one of the four cardinal virtues of the ancient Greek Stoic philosophers and was always depicted as a woman, but this figure could also derive from Athena/Minerva, the goddess of wisdom. The twin pillars behind her symbolize good and evil, and upholding of the law.

The double-edged sword represents one edge to condemn and the other to save. It can also refer to both sides of an argument, and farther back to the double meanings of the Delphic oracles. The sword could also be an echo of Minerva, who is said to have sprung fully armed from the brain of Jupiter, and is portrayed in military apparel.

The scales symbolize the weighing of good and evil, based on the belief that no amount of wrong can possibly outweigh even a little right.

The dual aspects of Justice are repeatedly emphasized in her symbols, which all come in pairs, including her double crown. Here the two parts of the crown are clearly differentiated and fairly plain, but some decks adorn Justice with elaborate, two-tier, turreted headgear.

Justice, or Adjustment, balances opposites to achieve equilibrium.

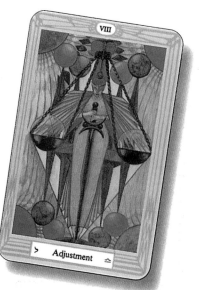

The Hermit

This card absorbs some of its meaning from the cards around it. It can mean enlightenment and the voice of the inner self, a journey that teaches something of value, delayed attainment, and the need to choose an unfamiliar path. If reversed, it can denote a closed mind, a perfectionist, excessive caution, and a reluctance to grow up.

SUGGESTED READING

1 Upright or Reversed Hermit
The querent must travel by own inner light to find direction in life.

2 Upright or Reversed Hermit
Wise counsel and support is given.

3 Upright Hermit
A time of delay or slowing down must be accepted.
Reversed Hermit
Do not shut out the world through fear of the unknown.

4 Upright Hermit
Beginning to find direction and fix goals.
Reversed Hermit
Do not be too. proud to ask others for help.

5 Upright Hermit
Self-sufficiency and inner beliefs bring happiness.
Reversed Hermit
Possible journey which could bring something of value.

6 Upright Hermit
A sudden flash of insight shows the right way.
Reversed Hermit
Closed minds give no chance of personal growth.

7 Upright Hermit
Finding way out of dark woods by not taking well-trodden paths.
Reversed Hermit
Changed attitudes mean a changed life.

8 Upright Hermit
Knowing oneself brings understanding of others.
Reversed Hermit
Don't be like Peter Pan. Learn to face important issues and acknowledge own faults.

9 Upright Hermit
Do not listen to others; your own inner light shows the way forward.
Reversed Hermit
Being a perfectionist sometimes loses friends.

10 Upright Hermit
Life has put you to the test, and you have topped the class.
Reversed Hermit
No progress without careful planning. Man of spiritual wisdom and principle will influence your future life.

Spread diagram

5
Possible goal or destiny

10
The final outcome

1
2
Immediate influences
Present position of querent

9
Querent's hopes and ideals

4
Past influences

6
Future influences

8
Family and friends

3
Recent influences

7
Querent's negative feelings

Combinations of Cards

If this card is followed by the High Priestess, a secret will never be revealed. If the Priestess comes first, the secret will be discovered. If the Devil precedes the Hermit, his power will prevail, but if the Hermit comes first, he will shine light on underhand methods and powerful enemies, so that good will prevail. If the Hermit is reversed, the same outcomes will occur but be delayed.

The elderly Hermit journeys onward, supported by his staff and guided by his lantern.

The lantern is a symbol of the inner light that guides the traveler onto the right path. It represents the light of the divine spirit, leading the traveler onward in the search for wisdom and truth. Some see in the lamp a reference to Saturn as the planet of gloom, but modern astrologers personify Saturn as the archetypal schoolmaster, concealing a warm heart beneath a cold exterior.

The staff is the Hermit's support, and represents the strength of the divine spirit on which he can rely to keep a straight path. Cloaked with discretion and leaning on his faithful staff, he journeys through life slowly and deliberately, letting no one deflect him from his course. In early decks, he was depicted with numerous symbols of time and its passing, such as a stag for longevity, various chronological instruments, and the hourglass and reaping hook of Old Father Time.

Often depicted as a beggar or friar – his age and his beard denoting wisdom – the Hermit originated as Kronos, the Greek god of time, whom the Romans knew as Saturn, and who is more familiar to us as Old Father Time. The curved hood may be an echo of the symbolic scythe that Old Father Time carried.

The Hermit travels slowly but surely, spreading enlightenment from the sun at the center of his lamp.

The Wheel of Fortune

Fortune's wheel is a symbol of destiny and the eternal processes that underlie human existence. It implies cause and effect, the results of past actions, wisdom from experience, and can denote a new life, a creative breakthrough, or wealth. Reversed, it indicates excessive love of possessions, failed enterprise, and difficult change.

SUGGESTED READING

5 Possible goal or destiny

10 The final outcome

1 Immediate influences

2 Present position of querent

4 Past influences

6 Future influences

9 Querent's hopes and ideals

8 Family and friends

3 Recent influences

7 Querent's negative feelings

1 **Upright or Reversed Wheel**
A sudden stroke of good or bad luck.

2 **Upright or Reversed Wheel**
Victorious change.

3 **Upright Wheel**
Future success depends on past actions.
Reversed Wheel
Past waste of energies and talents affects future.

4 **Upright Wheel**
Change must be accepted before progress can be made.
Reversed Wheel
Beware that ostentation and material comfort have not become all-important.

5 **Upright Wheel**
Ongoing pattern of opportunities and changes.
Reversed Wheel
Examine all new offers and factors before discarding.

6 **Upright Wheel**
Sudden change in thinking or direction brings growth and happiness.
Reversed Wheel
Learn to give and receive.

7 **Upright Wheel**
Be philosophical; spiritual growth and wisdom comes from lessons learned.
Reversed Wheel
Learn to let go; do not cling to outworn concepts.

8 **Upright Wheel**
Maintain equilibrium; neither good nor bad luck is permanent.
Reversed Wheel
Be careful you are not neglecting talents.

9 **Upright Wheel**
A sudden change will occur; be ready for it.
Reversed Wheel
Success in life should never be measured solely in terms of possessions or other worldly achievements.

10 **Upright Wheel**
Opportunity for creative or artistic endeavor brings great success or beneficial change in life.
Reversed Wheel
The unexpected element alters plan's completion.

Combinations of Cards

It is a sign of lasting good fortune if the Cobbler, Hermit, High Priestess, or World appear near this card. When near the Cobbler, there will be an exciting change of profession, dwelling, or direction in life; with the World, light will be shed on hidden factors, bringing success; near the Priestess, there will be an artistic or scientific triumph. If the Chariot is next to the Wheel, it means triumph.

A half-human creature surveys the hapless figures clinging to the wheel of fate.

The winged and crowned figure, sitting at the top of the wheel and holding a scepter, is thought to be Osiris, the Egyptian god of the dead and of the afterlife and resurrection.

LA·ROUE·DE·FORTUNE

The wheel may derive from Ixion, a king of Greek legend who was bound to a fiery wheel to revolve for eternity in the infernal regions following his dalliance with Hera, the wife of Zeus. A popular medieval concept of hell was a wheel hung with the souls of the damned and rotated with apparent relish by Satan.

The monkey-like figure of the god Set, who was regarded as the incarnation of evil, crawls down the wheel, representing declining fortunes.

Creeping toward Osiris on the rim of the wheel, his fortunes rising, is the jackal-headed god Anubis, who escorted the dead before the judge of the infernal regions. He could also be seen as a symbol of renewed life and of the triumph of good.

The creature at the base of the wheel holds an Egyptian ankh, a symbol of eternal life, suggesting the possibility of redemption.

Strength

This is the most fortunate card in the deck: it affects all of the cards that appear with it, and has no strongly negative meanings. It stands for triumph of the spirit over the material, of love over hate, and of positive forces over negative. It can imply strength of character, power used wisely, and opportunity for the courageous.

5 Possible goal or destiny		**10** The final outcome
1		**9** Querent's hopes and ideals
4 Past influences	**2** Immediate influences — Present position of querent	**6** Future influences
		8 Family and friends
3 Recent influences		**7** Querent's negative feelings

Combinations of Cards

This card is so strong that it influences the entire layout. When followed by Death, it means illness – serious but not fatal. When Death precedes Strength, there will be an abrupt ending; if both these cards are reversed, there will be a narrow escape. If Strength comes before the Chariot, triumph will follow considerable effort. If the Chariot comes first, it means great strength in future trials.

SUGGESTED READING

1 Upright or Reversed Strength
Querent has integrity, self-discipline, self-knowledge, and creative energy, and is at a momentous time in life.

2 Upright or Reversed Strength
An offer which will change the future should not be refused.

3 Upright Strength
Querent has achieved mental balance and inner strength despite past trials.
Reversed Strength
Lack of self-confidence could delay eventual success.

4 Upright Strength
Latent creative or artistic potential realized.
Reversed Strength
Control of own anger and pride will bring victory.

5 Upright Strength
Wonderful offer coming, enabling important plans to be put into action.
Reversed Strength
Unreasonable demands; selfish and envious people must be firmly dealt with.

6 Upright Strength
Release of creative energy or realization of self-worth will change life.
Reversed Strength
Stand fast and have courage.

7 Upright Strength
Use ego more to build reputation. Too impartial and often self-denigrating.
Reversed Strength
Beware of a tendency to overindulge; curb appetites.

8 Upright Strength
Have courage of own convictions, and take a leap in the dark.
Reversed Strength
Do not let negative people affect you.

9 Upright Strength
Intelligent use of force and determination allied with talent brings success.
Reversed Strength
Overdominance in partnerships can often result in division.

10 Upright Strength
A wonderful chance to change life is on its way.
Reversed Strength
Your strength is as the strength of ten.

Strength, with her hands in the lion's mouth, shows the dominance of force allied to spirit.

LA FORCE

Strength is thought to be Cyrene, handmaiden of Artemis/Diana, the moon goddess. She was wrestling barehanded with a lion when she was carried off by the Sun, and later gave birth to Aristaeus, the huntsman god. She is depicted either opening or closing the jaws of an apparently tame lion. Ancient occultists believed that certain people possessed magical powers over animals, and a talisman similar to this card was used to bind men to beasts. The lion, symbolizing the sun and the masculine principle, was often linked with the unicorn, a symbol of the moon and virginity.

In some decks, she is dressed plainly, to denote purity, and has no adornment other than a hat or crown. In others, such as the Rider-Waite deck (where this card is number eight to fit the numerical system of the cabala), she wears a white robe to denote purity, and has roses in her hair and at her waist, representing the invincible union of desires and spiritual strength.

The figure of Strength – also known as Fortitude or the Enchantress – wears a wide-brimmed hat in the shape of a figure eight, similar to that worn by the Cobbler. The hat describes the flowing shape of the cosmic lemniscate, the symbol used by the ancient Egyptians to signify immortality.

Strength, or Lust, easily reins in the lion while holding a full cup aloft, representing passion and joy in her dominance.

Lust

The Hanged Man

The theme of this card is willing sacrifice, entailing hardship — perhaps the renunciation of intellectual superiority or of hatred. It can imply stamina, foresight, a spiritual decision that brings serenity, and occult power. Reversed, it can mean futile sacrifice, selfishness, and irresponsibility.

5 Possible goal or destiny			**10** The final outcome
	1 **2** Immediate influences Present position of querent	**6** Future influences	**9** Querent's hopes and ideals
4 Past influences			**8** Family and friends
	3 Recent influences		**7** Querent's negative feelings

SUGGESTED READING

1 Upright or Reversed Hanged Man
Querent has great foresight and stamina and is aware of a higher power.

2 Upright or Reversed Hanged Man
A pause in affairs or a sacrifice which will benefit later.

3 Upright Hanged Man
Sacrifice will be made, or has already been made, that is spiritually enriching.
Reversed Hanged Man
Have let things slip or go downhill through a low sense of self-worth.

4 Upright Hanged Man
A relationship which must be sacrificed or viewed in a new way.
Reversed Hanged Man
Someone may make unrealistic promises.

5 Upright Hanged Man
Be assured of a higher power bringing inner peace.
Reversed Hanged Man
Resolutions not followed through bring inner conflict.

6 Upright Hanged Man
Make new goals and wait for the right moment to forge ahead.
Reversed Hanged Man
Look beyond the present.

7 Upright Hanged Man
Recognize and change old behavior patterns.
Reversed Hanged Man
Escaping responsibilities brings a false sense of security.

8 Upright Hanged Man
Take care not to see act of giving help as more important than person being helped.
Reversed Hanged Man
Sacrifices are often made through an overdeveloped sense of duty.

9 Upright Hanged Man
A turning point in spiritual life means trust, forgiveness, and contentment.
Reversed Hanged Man
Intuition and prophetic power is developing; use it wisely.

10 Upright Hanged Man
Things that are hidden will eventuate and bring change for the better.
Reversed Hanged Man
You have sacrificed too often. Get on with own life.

Combinations of Cards

The Hanged Man and Temperance next to each other mean deception, false promises, and indecision. The Hanged Man and Death signify a major sacrifice, or ending something with regret. If the Devil is seen with this card, it means a partnership, bond, or marriage, in which one partner makes a big sacrifice to ensure contentment, and a partner who is selfish must be prepared to give more.

Hands in pockets, the Hanged Man endures his self–imposed sacrifice with serenity.

The man's face seems nonchalant or entranced. The figure may have originated from the worship of Dionysus/Bacchus and the Orphic mystery rites that celebrated sacrifice in order to achieve regeneration.

His legs form a cross. Depictions by medieval artists linked the Orphic theme with the story of Jesus, and depicted the Hanged Man as Judas Iscariot, with thirty pieces of silver tumbling from his pockets. Modern cards portray the falling coins as a symbol of contempt for worldly riches.

The Hanged Man is bound and suspended by his left heel, a form of public disgrace, known as "bafflement," which was used in Renaissance times, notably to humiliate miscreant knights.

It was common practice to hang the "baffled" criminal from a tree, but here a makeshift gallows has been built between two saplings, each with six amputated branches, suggesting the possibility of renewed growth to come.

Although depicted as a crucified figure, the Hanged Man is bound to an Egyptian ankh, a symbol of life

The Hanged Man

Death

This is a deeply spiritual card which does not necessarily denote death, but can mean the end of an old life and a rebirth of the soul, a new awareness, a fresh start, creative talent realized, an unendurable situation ended. If reversed, it can mean loss of pretensions, fear of change, stagnation, and enforced sacrifice.

	5 Possible goal or destiny		10 The final outcome
4 Past influences	1 2 Immediate influences / Present position of querent	6 Future influences	9 Querent's hopes and ideals
	3 Recent influences		8 Family and friends
			7 Querent's negative feelings

Combinations of Cards

This card can indicate developments on a national scale as well as an individual one. When Death comes with the Tower, it could denote disaster or crisis, but if the Tower is reversed, there will be a narrow escape from calamity. If Death is followed by the World, it could mean the fall of a national leader or a world epidemic. If Death follows the Lovers, it denotes the end of a marriage or romance.

SUGGESTED READING

1 Upright or Reversed Death
The querent is about to undergo a transformation of ideas concerning either work or relationships.

2 Upright or Reversed Death
A sudden major event is in the offing.

3 Upright Death
The end of an era.
Reversed Death
Opportunity for transformation could be lost because of being bound by material possessions.

4 Upright Death
Something has come to an end. Acknowledge that all things change.
Reversed Death
Depression and self-loathing are negative and must be conquered to enable transformation to take place.

5 Upright Death
Snakes shed their skins; it's time to shed old concepts and face a new existence.
Reversed Death
Present attitude is causing feelings of stagnation. A change brings benefit.

6 Upright Death
Look at life in a new way to move onward.
Reversed Death
Change of view from the personal to the universal will achieve understanding.

7 Upright Death
Stop doubting own abilities and live fully.
Reversed Death
Pretensions will be stripped away through change.

8 Upright Death
The enforced removal of something that should have been relinquished freely.
Reversed Death
Fear of material insecurity has its basis in lack of faith in self.

9 Upright Death
External changes lead to transformation.
Reversed Death
Termination of unendurable situation brings hope.

10 Upright Death
The old and outworn has vanished, the new and better is on horizon.
Reversed Death
Nothing appears until dreaming stops and positive action begins.

A skeletal Death gathers his grisly harvest, but, prepares the way for renewal.

His sinister harvest includes hands, feet, and whitened bones, and some of the hands seem vainly to beseech his mercy. Yet the field is fertile; numerous shoots can be seen beneath the earth, and plants are beginning to flourish above – symbolizing regeneration, new growth, and that out of death comes life.

This card could hark back to Moira – Fate or Necessity – who was the supreme ruler of destiny. Despite its macabre appearance, most modern occultists interpret it as a sign of transformation.

The grim reaper's scythe represents the harvest. In medieval times this card was associated with the story of the harrowing of hell, when Christ was said to harvest souls from the very gates of hell.

Death waits for no one, and the decapitated heads show that he makes no distinction between the young and the old, the rulers and the ruled His disregard for rank is emphasized by the crown on one head, and the foot that crushes the other highlights the implacability of fate that does not spare even the child.

Death performs. a macabre dance; but all the while he reaps swirling bubbles of new life with his scythe.

Temperance

This card not only denotes moderation and compromise, even temperament, and humanity, but also the harmonizing of the spiritual and material, radiant energy, inspiration, creative genius, and often a rich marriage. Its reversed meanings include ill-advised action, clashing interests, and emotional instability.

SUGGESTED READING

1 Upright or Reversed Temperance
Querent looks for the best in others and sees both sides of a matter. Faces a new life.

2 Upright or Reversed Temperance
What has been imagined will come to pass, a dream comes true, or a favorable judgment in law ends a stalemate.

3 Upright Temperance
Harmonizing of material and psychic elements in life.
Reversed Temperance
Happiness is elusive; look inside yourself.

4 Upright Temperance
Working in harmony with others.
Reversed Temperance
Learn to compromise; do not push things too far.

5 Upright Temperance
A significant breakthrough in inspiration brings artistic triumph.
Reversed Temperance
Overemphasis on pursuing personal goals, or time spent in artistic pursuit, will damage a relationship.

6 Upright Temperance
Moderation and control in all affairs.
Reversed Temperance
Need to learn to adapt to changing circumstances.

7 Upright Temperance
Need to demonstrate feelings more in relationships.
Reversed Temperance
Emotional imbalance can result in a parting of the ways.

8 Upright Temperance
A wealthy partnership or marriage.
Reversed Temperance
Clashing interests and differing values could break up a relationship.

9 Upright Temperance
Radiant energy and ability to adapt bring success.
Reversed Temperance
Mood swings can result in unstable efforts; learn to control the emotions.

10 Upright Temperance
The final outcome of a matter will lead to a new chapter in life.
Reversed Temperance
Hesitating to make a decision will delay happiness.

Card Layout

5 — Possible goal or destiny

10 — The final outcome

1 —
2 — Immediate influences — Present position of querent

9 — Querent's hopes and ideals

4 — Past influences

6 — Future influences

8 — Family and friends

3 — Recent influences

7 — Querent's negative feelings

Combinations of Cards

Temperance preceding Justice means a long legal process resulting in equity and justice. If Justice comes first, there will be delays and the matter may not eventuate. However, when Temperance is reversed following Justice, it means an end to hesitation. When Temperance comes next to the Lovers, it means indecision; if the Lovers is reversed, it means deceit on the part of the lover.

Temperance is seen blending and harmonizing; hers is the elixir of grace and inspiration.

Temperance unites heaven, or the spiritual, and earth, or the material, represented by mountains and plants. Some decks add a pool at her feet as a symbol of spirituality.

The liquid symbolizes cleansing, strengthening, and inspiration. Pouring it from one vessel into the other is thought to mean the purifying of the soul by spiritual grace. The liquid is considered to be the essence of the mind, so the spiritual nourishment acts upon those who are materially minded to bring them inspiration.

The winged female figure wears a flower on her forehead, possibly a rose, the symbol of perfection. Other decks make her more definitely an angel, and some replace the flower with an emblem such as a solar sign.

This card may derive from Aquarius, the water bearer, or from Dionysus/Bacchus performing the ancient rite of mixing water and wine. Some think the figure represents Ganymede, the cupbearer of the gods, whose duty was to refill the empty cup with the nectar of immortality.

Temperance; or Art, is depicted as the androgynous figure of two united lovers, blending the elements.

The Devil

A powerful and largely negative card, the Devil can imply carnal excess, self-indulgence, greed, destruction, and sudden, inexorable events, but it can also indicate energy, humor, and sensuality, and its outcome can depend on other cards. If reversed, it can be favorable, meaning liberation and healing.

SUGGESTED READING

1 Upright or Reversed Devil
Querent has humor, vitality, sexuality, and creative power, but must avoid excess in physical appetites.

2 Upright or Reversed Devil
Sudden, inexorable event for good or ill, which querent cannot influence or control.

3 Upright Devil
A wrong choice could have been made which will require self-discipline.
Reversed Devil
Confronting and accepting own faults brings about a happier beginning.

4 Upright Devil
When negative influences are removed, rapid progress will be made.
Reversed Devil
There is a feeling of traveling down a one-way street alone.

5 Upright Devil
Courage will enable escape from a dangerous or damaging situation.
Reversed Devil
A shock reveals inner persona and begins the process of spiritual enlightenment.

6 Upright Devil
Querent is about to discard false image or mask.
Reversed Devil
Creative power is unused due to negative view of self.

7 Upright Devil
Do not allow physical aspect of life to dominate.
Reversed Devil
Excessive pressure can be caused by own intolerance and selfishness.

8 Upright Devil
Ensure that extravagance does not cause you to live beyond your means.
Reversed Devil
It is time to make amends to those you have hurt.

9 Upright Devil
Learn to like and accept yourself for what you are.
Reversed Devil
Success and personal happiness come from hard work and inner struggle.

10 Upright Devil
A sudden change in life will happen shortly.
Reversed Devil
Happiness and creative success are a reward for courage and self-honesty.

Spread positions

- **5** Possible goal or destiny
- **10** The final outcome
- **1** / **2** Immediate influences / Present position of querent
- **4** Past influences
- **6** Future influences
- **9** Querent's hopes and ideals
- **8** Family and friends
- **3** Recent influences
- **7** Querent's negative feelings

Combinations of Cards

When the Hierophant and Devil appear in a spread, they negate each other, and the surrounding cards will decide the outcome. If the Devil precedes the Emperor, it can mean national agitation; if the Emperor comes first, it can denote threat to a powerful leader. If the Devil precedes Justice, there will be a miscarriage of justice, but if Justice comes first, the accusation will be proved false.

The horned and winged Devil portrays evil, but hints at the chance of redemption.

The horned and helmeted imps are depicted as male and female figures, and are thought to be bestialized versions of the Lovers, suggesting perhaps the consequences of unbridled carnal passion. But their neck chains are loose, implying that strength of mind and spirit could conquer evil and free them from bondage.

A figure resembling this medieval Christian concept of Satan was worshiped in a cult with links to Mithras, Dionysus, and Saturn. It was often carved with one or more human or animal faces, glowing eyes, stag's horns, wings, and bird's claws.

The breastplate could be an echo of the cords or serpents that were often depicted entwining the idol's body. They suggest human bondage to evil, and the difficulty of escaping its constraints.

His eagle's claw feet are firmly astride a pedestal or mock throne, symbolizing worldly domination. Other decks replace the claws with the cloven hooves of Satan. The Devil stands in opposition to the Cobbler, bearing a sword instead of a wand and raising his right hand.

The Devil, depicted as a goat with spiraling horns, represents creative energy but also greed and excess.

The Tower

Sudden change is the keynote of this card. It can mean unexpected shock or catastrophe and shattered illusions, but also the flash of inspiration, and an opportunity that leads to happiness. It is stronger when reversed, implying the downfall of the selfish, destroyed ambition, imprisonment, or a broken partnership.

SUGGESTED READING

5 Possible goal or destiny

I Immediate influences / **2** Present position of querent

4 Past influences

6 Future influences

3 Recent influences

10 The final outcome

9 Querent's hopes and ideals

8 Family and friends

7 Querent's negative feelings

I Upright or Reversed Tower
This card denotes a change for the better after a sudden disappointment or loss.

2 Upright or Reversed Tower
Something has now reached boiling point.

3 Upright Tower
The old must be destroyed to make way for the new.
Reversed Tower
Lack of insight, ego, and pride could prevent making necessary changes.

4 Upright Tower
Ambition was built on weak foundations or false promises from others.
Reversed Tower
Self-knowledge and honesty can separate the true from the false; self-evaluation can bring contentment.

5 Upright Tower
Do what is right and happiness will prevail.
Reversed Tower
Self-knowledge brings about a traumatic but nonetheless satisfying change.

6 Upright Tower
Look at things as they are, not as you would like them to be.
Reversed Tower
See the writing on the wall; know that present confines must change.

7 Upright Tower
New inner awareness results from sudden conflict.
Reversed Tower
Take what you want, but you must pay for it.

8 Upright Tower
Relationships flounder and need to be restructured.
Reversed Tower
Spur-of-the-moment action could bring chaos and conflict.

9 Upright Tower
Let it go, don't fight it!
Reversed Tower
A high cost must be paid to gain freedom of mind, body, and spirit.

10 Upright Tower
The change or blow coming will eventually bring happiness and healing.
Reversed Tower
Wonderful opportunities are coming soon.

Combinations of Cards

If it precedes the High Priestess, the Tower means disaster in the sphere of religion or in an established institution. If both these cards are reversed, it can mean injuries to the brain, a mental breakdown, and consequent physical collapse. If Strength appears in the spread, it adds potency to the Tower's meaning; if the World is present, it makes the outcome a general rather than a personal matter.

The brick tower is struck by lightning, but the victims cast from its windows are survivors.

The two figures thrown from the tower indicate the reversal of existing structures and contact of the spiritual (the head) with the material (the earth). One has already recovered sufficiently to reach for a plant, a symbol of life, signifying the destruction of the old making way for the new.

The elaborate gold and red feather is a stylized lightning bolt. It refers to the myth of the Titans, giants who tore Dionysus to pieces and were blasted by divine lightning. Like the Phoenix, Dionysus arose from the ashes, assuming the persona of Bacchus.

Shapes like cannon balls surround the tower and float to the ground. These are thought to be Hebrew yods, the symbols of spiritual matter descending into the material world.

The turreted top of the tower resembles a crown, reinforcing the idea of greatness and ambition overthrown. The entry of the lightning beneath the crown could also signify enlightenment, or a cleansing catharsis.

An all seeing eye watches over the destinies of those falling from the tower into the cathartic flames below.

The Star

Hope, love, and rebirth are the themes of this card. It indicates love of humanity, optimism, friendship reciprocated, firm promises, good health, insight, and guidance from above. If reversed, it can mean over-optimism and trust, intolerance, procrastination, pessimism, and lack of self-esteem.

5 Possible goal or destiny		**10** The final outcome
1 / **2** Immediate influences / Present position of querent	**6** Future influences	**9** Querent's hopes and ideals
4 Past influences		**8** Family and friends
3 Recent influences		**7** Querent's negative feelings

Combinations of Cards

If the Star precedes the Empress, it denotes a happy, ordered, and tranquil existence. If the Cobbler follows the Star, this augurs a happy beginning for a new project or artistic venture. If the Empress comes before the Star, success will be assured through strong ambition and sustained effort. If the Star appears next to the Devil in any position, they cancel each other out.

SUGGESTED READING

1 Upright or Reversed Star
Joyous and positive with a strong faith in the future. If disappointed in love, someone worthy will come into life.

2 Upright or Reversed Star
Balance and restraint when facing problems help to bring a happy solution.

3 Upright Star
Positive energy for fruitful future action. God helps those who help themselves.
Reversed Star
Sometimes one has to learn not to give so much.

4 Upright Star
Peace through struggle; good friends and inner strength.
Reversed Star
Do not become intolerant of or feel superior to those who do not possess your intellect or experience.

5 Upright Star
Courage and self-belief bring triumph and success.
Reversed Star
If inner voice is ignored, success will be delayed.

6 Upright Star
A renewal of mental, physical, and spiritual energy.
Reversed Star
Do not allow others to put you down; have confidence.

7 Upright Star
All fears are outweighed by courage and positivity.
Reversed Star
Self-doubt could impede progress temporarily, but confidence will be restored.

8 Upright Star
Encouragement and help given; harmonious atmosphere will prevail.
Reversed Star
Looking only at the positive in life can weaken ability to confront the negative.

9 Upright Star
Harmony will only come when a decision which has been put off is made.
Reversed Star
A course of action may hurt others but is necessary.

10 Upright or Reversed Star
You have taken the right path or made the right decision, despite the cost. Happiness and real love await you.

The nude maiden kneeling by a pool beneath the stars personifies bright optimism and love.

She pours water from two pitchers. One is said to contain the waters of life, replenishing the material plane, and the other the waters of universal consciousness, refreshing mind and spirit, and refilling the pool of memory. Her rule over both dimensions is symbolized by having one foot on land and the other foot in water.

The female figure may represent Venus, the lode star of the ancient Greeks, who named her Hesperus when she followed the sun as an evening star, and Lucifer or Phosphorus (light-bringer) at dawn.

The eight-pointed star above her is known as the star of Innana, from ancient Sumerian legend, believed to represent cosmic light and energy. It is surrounded by a constellation of seven smaller stars, thought to depict the Pleiades.

Behind her are trees with lush green leaves, denoting spring. A bird, symbol of love, sits on one, and another perches near her outstretched foot.

Rebirth and hope are symbolized by the spiraling star and the female figure replenishing the material and spiritual worlds.

67

The Moon

This is a card with strong links to the subconscious. It can imply intuition, imagination, and creativity, but it may mean uncertainty, fluctuation, deception, and spite. When reversed, its effects are weakened. It can mean storms weathered and success gained, but may indicate an emotional crisis.

SUGGESTED READING

1 **Upright or Reversed Moon**
Creative, imaginative, and sometimes overemotional, with hidden depths of feeling, intuition, and psychic ability..

2 **Upright or Reversed Moon**
A relationship issue to be resolved, or a creative project about to begin.

3 **Upright Moon**
Meditate; beware of own subconscious motivation.
Reversed Moon
Do not be deceived by false promises from others; situation can be illusory.

4 **Upright Moon**
A period of fluctuation and uncertainty.
Reversed Moon
Fear of insecurity can prevent spiritual transformation.

5 **Upright Moon**
Storms weathered, success and stability gained.
Reversed Moon
Be aware that emotions can sometimes mislead.

6 **Upright Moon**
After a storm there is often a rainbow.
Reversed Moon
Learn to trust inner voices and gain self-confidence.

7 **Upright Moon**
Imagination could run riot and obscure clear vision.
Reversed Moon
Possibility of deception, misunderstandings, or false accusations by others.

8 **Upright Moon**
Lesson learned through consequences of past actions.
Reversed Moon
Consequences of past actions are completed as relationships resurface.

9 **Upright Moon**
Creative work fueled by subconscious and dreams.
Reversed Moon
A mystery is solved and you forge ahead.

10 **Upright Moon**
Imagination harnessed to practicality brings artistic success.
Reversed Moon
The final testing of some matter; let your intuition be your guide.

Spread positions

- **5** Possible goal or destiny
- **10** The final outcome
- **1** / **2** Immediate influences — Present position of querent
- **4** Past influences
- **6** Future influences
- **9** Querent's hopes and ideals
- **8** Family and friends
- **3** Recent Influences
- **7** Querent's negative feelings

Combinations of Cards

The Moon has a strong malign influence when next to the Tower, the Devil, or Justice, implying unjustness and deceit. The Moon followed by Death could mean loss as a result of slander, but if both cards are reversed, the truth will be discovered. If the Moon comes before the Lovers, it can mean the end of a love affair through deception or lies, or an illusion of love which ends abruptly.

The crescent, half, and full moon shed shifting light on the symbolic creatures of land and sea.

The Moon is depicted in all three phases, symbolizing the mental, emotional, and spiritual levels. The face is thought to be that of the moon goddess Artemis/Diana, although some link her with Hecate, triple goddess of the moon, with powers over heaven and hell, earth and sea.

Rays or droplets of dew fall almost into the mouths of the hounds. These may refer to spiritual light entering the imagination and feeding the mind.

Diana was also the huntress, and the dogs crouched by a deep pond, baying to their goddess, could be her hounds, who stood guard at the pillars to the underworld – possibly represented here by the turreted forts.

The creature rising from the depths is based on the crab, the astrological symbol associated with the Moon, which governs the sea and tides and all aquatic creatures. The Moon was also said to rule all reflecting surfaces, and was itself considered to be a mirror, symbolizing the reflected light of the inner mind.

Jackals guard the threshold between knowledge and ignorance under the fluctuating light of the moon.

The Sun

Success and happiness are the themes of this card. It can denote health, opportunity, triumph through energy, especially in art and science, gratitude, and wealth. Although weakened when reversed, it is never strongly negative, but can signify a need for self-knowledge or a lack of confidence.

SUGGESTED READING

1 Upright or Reversed Sun
Querent possesses optimism, positive energy, the ability to succeed, and also to give and receive love.

2 Upright or Reversed Sun
Happiness and contentment in new friendship or relationship.

3 Upright Sun
Past successful accomplishments bring future joys and rewards.
Reversed Sun
Investigate every aspect of a new project.

4 Upright Sun
Work or study brings triumph and reward.
Reversed Sun
Loss of work or a broken relationship will result in gain.

5 Upright Sun
A triumphant new beginning as a result of past endeavor and effort.
Reversed Sun
Be honest with yourself; need for self-realism.

6 Upright Sun
Don't hesitate; take the opportunity coming with both hands.
Reversed Sun
Disappointment because of a sudden cancellation.

7 Upright Sun
Happiness is already in your heart, not just around the corner.
Reversed Sun
Real effort is needed, not daydreaming, to reach goal.

8 Upright Sun
Never give in! Failure is not for you.
Reversed Sun
A deceptive person could take advantage of a trusting nature.

9 Upright Sun
Either a fulfilled romantic relationship or a triumph of achievement.
Reversed Sun
Give thanks for your blessings. There will be many more.

10 Upright Sun
There will be future joy and happiness despite present struggle.
Reversed Sun
A happy reunion.

Spread positions:
5 Possible goal or destiny
1
2 Immediate influences
Present position of querent
4 Past influences
6 Future influences
3 Recent influences
10 The final outcome
9 Querent's hopes and ideals
8 Family and friends
7 Querent's negative feelings

Combinations of Cards

When the Sun precedes Death, there will be a triumph through something being ended. A death of some kind can bring benefit or vindication. When the Sun follows the Tower, good will come out of evil, and a sudden catastrophe proves of ultimate benefit. When the Sun appears with the Two of Cups, two happy people will share a loving, lasting partnership.

The mighty sun, shedding its warmth on two young boys, expresses joy and triumph.

To many of the ancients, the sun was a symbol of royalty. Egyptians and Romans carried sun talismans for protection and success. The cult of Dionysus celebrated the sun's birthday on December 25th – a date later absorbed into the Christian calendar.

The two boys, who could be twins, are enjoying the rewards of the sun's beneficence. In early decks, children are depicted running or playing beneath the sun. On some later cards, the figures are young lovers. Other decks show a person spinning or unwinding the thread of the sun's rays.

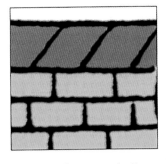

The wall may symbolize the protective powers of the sun, and its strength. Some decks show sunflowers peeping over a stone wall, to reinforce the connection with the sun.

Rayed with light, the sun drops the dew of its bounty upon the earth. Fire was believed to come from the sun, and was considered purifying and a safeguard against evil. The most sacred were "elf" fires, which occurred spontaneously as a result of the sun's rays.

The sun sheds light and happiness into all the signs of the zodiac, while children dance joyfully within its life-giving rays.

Judgment

This card has connotations of a life well spent. It can suggest rewards for past efforts, resolution, release, and renewal. Reversed, it can mean transient success, loss, bitterness, and fear of death, but its influence is weakened by proximity to physical cards, such as the Devil, Cobbler, or Wheel.

SUGGESTED READING

I **Upright or Reversed Judgment**
Querent is discriminating, discerning, self-critical, and analytical. May have lived the way others expected, not as he or she wanted to live.

2 **Upright or Reversed Judgment**
Something has come to an end and the future can now be faced realistically.

3 **Upright Judgment**
A worthy life; work has been well done.
Reversed Judgment
Time to break away from conventional thinking.

4 **Upright Judgment**
End of a chapter, and liberation from restriction.
Reversed Judgment
Confrontation with self-evasion and mistakes.

5 **Upright Judgment**
Creative efforts from the past bring future success.
Reversed Judgment
Favorable decision brings benefit from legal official.

6 **Upright Judgment**
Wonderful things are starting to happen which will bring fulfillment.
Reversed Judgment
Do not fear change or indulge in self-pity.

7 **Upright Judgment**
Understanding of past failures brings healing.
Reversed Judgment
Life's lessons, though painful, must be learned.

8 **Upright Judgment**
Need for a new location, new work, or new ideas.
Reversed Judgment
Unwanted ties must be broken for renewal to occur.

9 **Upright Judgment**
Can now see future and forge ahead.
Reversed Judgment
Looking for freedom but inability to find way out.

IO **Upright Judgment**
At last clear vision shows the true path.
Reversed Judgment
Lessons have been learned and happiness lies ahead.

Spread positions

5 — Possible goal or destiny

IO — The final outcome

I — Immediate influences

2 — Present position of querent

4 — Past influences

6 — Future influences

9 — Querent's hopes and ideals

8 — Family and friends

3 — Recent influences

7 — Querent's negative feelings

Combinations of Cards

This card is very powerful. Preceding the Chariot, it means fame and triumph. If the Chariot is reversed, the triumph will be shortlived, because the effect of the sudden success will weaken the character. If the Hermit follows Judgment, triumph will always be of an inner spiritual kind, or only apparent after death. If the Hermit is reversed, discoveries of great benefit will be made public.

An angel summons the dead to judgment, but they can look forward to rebirth in a new life.

LE · JUGEMENT

The angel is probably St. Michael, reputed to have brought humans the gift of prudence. He is said to be one of the archangels responsible for keeping the planets on their courses. His planet was Mercury, a god associated with guiding the dead.

Three figures have emerged from the grave: a young woman, an old man, and a figure shown from the back, who could represent the viewer of the card. They appear to be praying. Although they are naked, indicating that they can conceal nothing, their living form suggests redemption and rebirth.

The angel appears at the center of a spiraling, circular cloud, and the card shows repeated circular shapes, symbolizing the end and the beginning, the cycle of birth and death.

The trumpet is hung with a flag bearing the cross of St. Michael, and the angel blows it to open a grave. St. Michael was represented in medieval times as the angel who carried the scales at the "last trump," or final judgment, to weigh the souls of the risen dead.

The central childlike figure awaits the birth of a new age, or aeon, after the final judgment.

The World

This final card is seen by some as the best, with its meanings of completion and reward. It signifies celebration, triumphant conclusion, material and spiritual success, happiness, lessons learned, and also travel. Its reversed meanings largely concern lack of personal development and vision.

SUGGESTED READING

I **Upright or Reversed World**
Querent has worked hard and deserves the reward about to arrive, which brings inner peace and joy as a long-held dream comes true.

2 **Upright or Reversed World**
A welcome change of scene or a wish granted.

3 **Upright World**
A circle has been completed or work is finished.
Reversed World
Happiness cannot be measured in terms of society's approval.

4 **Upright World**
The freedom to accept new responsibilities.
Reversed World
Fear of change limits potential for success.

5 **Upright World**
A goal is reached or a wish becomes reality.
Reversed World
Always remember the effort required to attain success.

6 **Upright World**
Create a dream and it will come true.
Reversed World
Success will be delayed.

7 **Upright World**
It is time to share your dream with others.
Reversed World
Spiritual growth and renewal brings new values.

8 **Upright World**
Accept the ideas of others as equally valid.
Reversed World
Others rely on you for an important decision.

9 **Upright World**
Travel to new and exciting places.
Reversed World
Change could be prevented by overstrong attachment to person or place.

IO **Upright World**
A triumphant conclusion or the beginning of a dream come true.
Reversed World
Freedom to start afresh.

Spread positions

5 Possible goal or destiny

IO The final outcome

I

2 Immediate influences

Present position of querent

4 Past influences

6 Future influences

9 Querent's hopes and ideals

8 Family and friends

3 Recent influences

7 Querent's negative feelings

Combinations of Cards

If the World comes next to the Sun, it means an uplifting emotional experience, bringing joy, love, and harmony. If the World follows the Hanged Man, a loving sacrifice will bring a triumph. If the World comes first, it denotes a sacrifice that could result in sadness and parting. The World's essentially abstract quality is negated by the presence of Justice, the Hermit, or the Cobbler.

A dancing figure, wreathed in triumph, conveys joyous celebration and success.

LE · MONDE

A lion, a bull, an angel, and an eagle are usually depicted at the corners of this card. Sometimes a man replaces the angel. These are the four living creatures of the prophet Ezekiel, which also stood for the four cardinal points: north, south, east, and west (the direction of the poles, and also of sunrise and sunset).

The dancing female figure is thought to derive from the culmination of the Greek mystery rites, when the initiate who had successfully passed through ordeals was dressed in honor of the sun and presented to the populace. She is in direct contrast with the Hanged Man, and has the opposite (left) leg crossed behind her. The long, floating scarf is probably the Olympian stole which was bestowed upon the triumphant initiate. It is a symbol of well-won achievement.

A traditional emblem of victory, the wreath that surrounds the dancer could also be a reference to the mandala, a symbol of the universe, totality, or wholeness. It is bound in two places by ribbons, but some decks show four ties and replace the ribbons with roses.

At the center of the World, or Universe, a maiden joyfully dances Inside a wreath of stars.

The Universe

The

Minor Arcana

The minor arcana comprises four suits: Cups, Wands, Pentacles, and Swords. Each suit has fourteen cards: ace to ten, and four court cards – queen, king, knight, and a young person of either sex, known variously as the knave, page, or maid-of-honor. The court cards portray the influential people in the querent's life, but can also reveal the seeker's own attributes, which may be manifest or hidden. The numbered cards represent the experiences and decisions that can illuminate the querent's motives and suggest future directions he or she may take. The suit cards from the traditional Marseilles deck are shown throughout this section.

The Suit of Cups

Cups are linked to water, with its connotations of changeability and hidden depths. They are concerned with the subconscious mind and instincts, and with emotional development. Love, fulfillment, joy, and relationships are the province of Cups. Symbolized in most decks as chalices, Cups are thought to be associated with the Church and the holy grail (the legendary cup used by Jesus at the Last Supper). The association of Cups with creativity may derive from their relationship with the Church, and the role of the monastic scribes and artists of earlier times. Despite their spiritual dimension, however, they are closely connected with worldly happiness. The suit of Cups is usually more positive than negative, since it deals in the pleasant realms of love, dreams, and joyful emotions, rather than spiritual conflict or stark moral choice. This aspect is echoed in regular playing cards, where Cups become Hearts.

POSITIVE ASPECTS

Romance
*
Friendship
*
Physical Pleasure
*
Creativity
*
Sociability
*

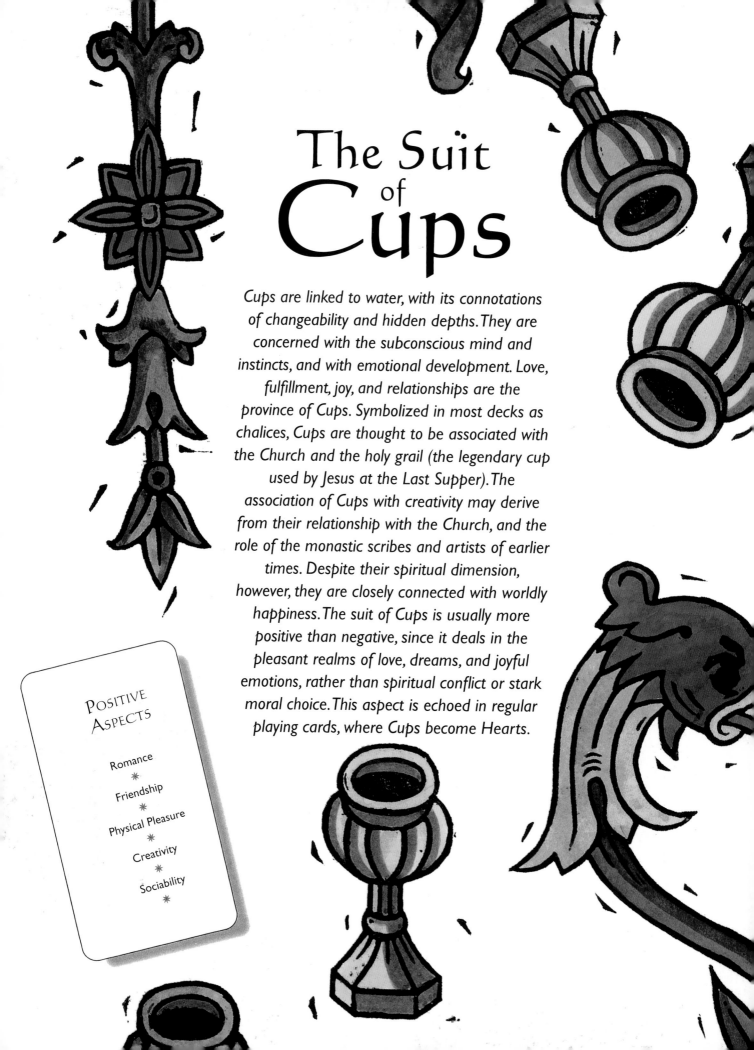

NEGATIVE
ASPECTS

Jealousy
*
Pain
*
Rejection
*
Too great a love of luxury
*
Preoccupation with self
*

King of Cups

ROY · DE · COUPE

A powerful, professional man, over 35, from any walk of life but often connected with law, education, or religion. He is reliable, and could give useful advice or act on behalf of the querent, but is also crafty, hides his emotions, and usually puts himself first.

SUGGESTED READING

1 **Upright or Reversed King**
An influential man, generous, worldly, a good partner, with sound ideas, but can be self-interested and manipulative. Can signify a skillful negotiator who helps the querent.

2 **Upright or Reversed King**
A powerful new friend or counselor who gives support.

3 **Upright King**
A deep-seated worry or problem reemerges.
Reversed King
Finding one's own solution can avoid open confrontation. or disagreement.

4 **Upright King**
The need for good, professional advice.
Reversed King
Pride could prevent the seeking of necessary guidance.

5 **Upright King**
Generous help brings a happy solution.
Reversed King
Guard against manipulation in financial or legal matters.

6 **Upright King**
Peace comes through the decision to seek advice.
Reversed King
Beware of deception in a financial matter.

7 **Upright King**
A good friend is not what he appears to be.
Reversed King
Know that those who counsel remain in control and so avoid being emotionally affected.

8 **Upright King**
A good friend who supports and advises.
Reversed King
The wrong time for new emotional entanglements.

9 **Upright King**
An intelligent professional man opens the door to a new opportunity.
Reversed King
Deception from a man who keeps his true feelings hidden.

10 **Upright King**
A favorable result is achieved with the help of a powerful man.
Reversed King
Make sure that you are seeing your problems realistically.

---

5 Possible goal or destiny

10 The final outcome

1

2 Immediate influences

Present position of querent

4 Past influences

6 Future influences

9 Querent's hopes and ideals

8 Family and friends

3 Recent influences

7 Querent's negative feelings

Queen of Cups

A sensitive, artistic woman with a loving disposition, the Queen of Cups is one who puts her ideals into practice. She is romantic and a good partner, but her reverse characteristics are perversity, unreliability, and dishonesty. She can indicate new horizons or romance.

REYNE · DE · COUPE

SUGGESTED READING

1 Upright or Reversed Queen
An intuitive, creative, highly emotional woman, who is honest and practical, and can turn her dreams into reality.

2 Upright or Reversed Queen
A woman enters life and reveals new possibilities.

3 Upright Queen
The deepening of inner knowledge aids self-development and awareness.
Reversed Queen
An urge to help others with their problems becomes of paramount importance.

4 Upright Queen
Long-awaited success is coming closer.
Reversed Queen
Rational thinkers can sometimes suffer through ignoring intuitive urges.

5 Upright Queen
Practical application of talents brings the realization of a dream.
Reversed Queen
Do not listen to others. Follow your heart and achieve the impossible.

6 Upright Queen
Help is available from a mature, discerning female.
Reversed Queen
When setting a target, take care that vital factors are not ignored.

7 Upright Queen
Acting on own intuition assures future success.
Reversed Queen
Deception from female who knows some secrets.

8 Upright Queen
Valuable insight into own motivation gained through a challenging female.
Reversed Queen
A close female friend shows lack of sympathy.

9 Upright Queen
A happy marriage or a dream realized.
Reversed Queen
Fulfillment in work must be balanced with one's inner emotional needs.

10 Upright Queen
Emotional fulfillment or professional success.
Reversed Queen
Emotional independence brought about by realization of own strength.

81

```
        5                       10
     Possible                 The final
     goal or                  outcome
     destiny

        1                       9
        2                    Querent's
     Immediate                 hopes
  4   influences      6       and ideals
 Past              Future
influences         influences    8
      Present                  Family
     position of                and
     querent                   friends

        3                       7
     Recent                  Querent's
    influences                negative
                              feelings
```

Knight of Cups

The Knight represents a young man, aged between 21 and 35, cultivated, sensual, and romantic. He could also be deceptive and possess an overdeveloped ego. He signifies a pleasant meeting or invitation, a lover or rival, or a deep relationship that must be worked through.

CAVALIER · DE · COUPE

SUGGESTED READING

1 Upright or Reversed Knight
A man of refined intellectual and artistic mind, or a bearer of sudden news.

2 Upright or Reversed Knight
An important offer or invitation comes suddenly.

3 Upright Knight
Great intellectual capacity and willpower shown.
Reversed Knight
Learn to be more flexible and open to new ideas.

4 Upright Knight
The beginning of a new project or idea.
Reversed Knight
Study a new proposition from all possible angles.

5 Upright Knight
A new goal is reached.
Reversed Knight
Check carefully before signing legal papers.

6 Upright Knight
A passionate conviction leads to progress in work.
Reversed Knight
Unrealistic goals may be set unless sensible limits are accepted and applied.

7 Upright Knight
Do not be afraid to give to a new love relationship.
Reversed Knight
Beware of subtle manipulation by a deceitful person.

8 Upright Knight
An invitation which could change the future.
Reversed Knight
A loved one has opposing views on a matter.

9 Upright Knight
Body, mind, and spirit all unite in ambition to succeed.
Reversed Knight
Success comes only after adapting ideas.

10 Upright Knight
Successful achievement or a deep, fulfilling relationship.
Reversed Knight
The necessity for learning to be emotionally flexible.

---

5 Possible goal or destiny

10 The final outcome

1

2 Immediate influences

Present position of querent

4 Past influences

6 Future influences

9 Querent's hopes and ideals

8 Family and friends

3 Recent influences

7 Querent's negative feelings

Knave of Cups

VALET·DE·COUPE

The Knave denotes a helpful person of either sex who is under 21. Melancholy, passionate, and imaginative, he or she can cause deception through excessive imagination. The Knave also means new business methods, and changes that will transform the future.

SUGGESTED READING

1 Upright or Reversed Knave
A loyal or meditative young person gives help or advice.

2 Upright or Reversed Knave
An important message or news of a birth.

3 Upright Knave
A new idea which needs to be developed.
Reversed Knave
Make sure your goals are realistic.

4 Upright Knave
Obstacles are gradually being removed.
Reversed Knave
Trust more in own intuition; it is an accurate guide.

5 Upright Knave
Realization of talents brings new approach to work or business.
Reversed Knave
When used wisely, emotions can fuel creative imagination.

6 Upright Knave
Be ready to seize new opportunity when it arrives.
Reversed Knave
The birth of new determination and pride.

7 Upright Knave
You must learn to love yourself before you can genuinely love another.
Reversed Knave
Learn to accept that nothing remains the same.

8 Upright Knave
A young friend sees the humor of life and teaches that laughter heals.
Reversed Knave
The fear of emotional vulnerability can lead to repression and unhappiness.

9 Upright Knave
Healing and a sense of inner renewal.
Reversed Knave
The discovery of a deception by a friend or close colleague.

10 Upright Knave
A new capacity to love comes after a time of hurt and rejection.
Reversed Knave
Waiting passively for happiness achieves nothing. Take action and create it.

	5 Possible goal or destiny		10 The final outcome
4 Past influences	1 / 2 Immediate influences / Present position of querent	6 Future influences	9 Querent's hopes and ideals
			8 Family and friends
	3 Recent influences		7 Querent's negative feelings

83

Ten of Cups

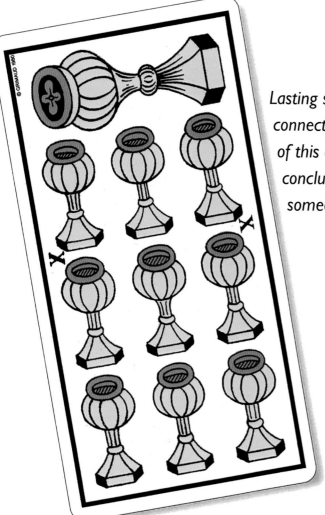

Lasting spiritual happiness, the love of friends, and success connected with work of a public nature are the province of this card. It can also mean a journey with a joyful conclusion. When reversed, it can mean a betrayal by someone close, or a fear of showing true feelings.

SUGGESTED READING

1 Upright or Reversed Ten
Happy family or loving friends bring spiritual contentment; or satisfaction comes from public work.

2 Upright or Reversed Ten
A sudden exciting occurrence or journey.

3 Upright Ten
Prestige and authority bring satisfaction.
Reversed Ten
An all-consuming passion is both self-destructive and dangerous to others.

4 Upright Ten
Living with passionate conviction and confidence.
Reversed Ten
Sadness caused by a family problem.

5 Upright Ten
The realization of a personal dream.
Reversed Ten
Inner security comes through a loving relationship.

6 Upright Ten
Financial success connected with property.
Reversed Ten
Feelings of regret over the loss of a friend.

7 Upright Ten
Do not be afraid to reveal true feelings.
Reversed Ten
An unhappy youth needs your peacemaking skills.

8 Upright Ten
A lifelong friendship is about to begin.
Reversed Ten
The betrayal by a friend is hard to accept.

9 Upright Ten
Permanence and stability in emotional life.
Reversed Ten
Acts of thoughtlessness and lack of consideration cause a deep rift to occur.

10 Upright Ten
Lasting domestic happiness, or prestige in public work.
Reversed Ten
Live your life truthfully in order to be happy.

---

5 Possible goal or destiny		10 The final outcome

	1			9 Querent's hopes and ideals
4 Past influences	2 Immediate influences Present position of querent	6 Future influences		8 Family and friends
	3 Recent influences			7 Querent's negative feelings

Nine of Cups

The material wish card of the minor arcana, its reversals are only mildly adverse. It can mean the fulfillment of a desire, emotional and material stability, good health, and generosity. When reversed, it can signify misplaced reliance on others, or overindulgence in food and drink.

SUGGESTED READING

1 Upright or Reversed Nine
Generosity, good health, and kindness abound.

2 Upright or Reversed Nine
Emotional and material stability and fulfillment.

3 Upright Nine
A soul at peace with itself will find true happiness.
Reversed Nine
Recognize own abilities and use them positively.

4 Upright Nine
The reward for sustained effort is coming.
Reversed Nine
To achieve success, follow your own innermost desires.

5 Upright Nine
Self-satisfaction and general contentment.
Reversed Nine
Avoid overindulgence in food and drink.

6 Upright Nine
Your goal is in sight.
Reversed Nine
Stress can be caused by attempting too much at once.

7 Upright Nine
Spiritual energy fuels a creative effort.
Reversed Nine
Progress becomes easier as worries diminish.

8 Upright Nine
Friends give valuable advice and support.
Reversed Nine
Be careful that others do not take advantage of your generous nature.

9 Upright Nine
Know your true purpose and follow your heart.
Reversed Nine
New and exciting plans suddenly materialize.

10 Upright Nine
The fulfillment of one overriding wish or desire.
Reversed Nine
Remember that happiness in life comes from appreciating what we already have.

	5 Possible goal or destiny		**10** The final outcome
	1		
4 Past influences	**2** Immediate influences / Present position of querent	**6** Future influences	**9** Querent's hopes and ideals
			8 Family and friends
	3 Recent Influences		**7** Querent's negative feelings

Eight of Cups

The card of the seeker of spiritual fulfillment, this signifies the need to seek a new life, or an attitude changed through disillusion. When reversed, the desire for sudden change can bring a difficult choice of direction, or disappointment in love because of fear of commitment.

SUGGESTED READING

1 **Upright or Reversed Eight**
The need to see the truth of a matter and realize that nothing can now change it.

2 **Upright or Reversed Eight**
Traveling somewhere new, mentally or physically.

3 **Upright Eight**
The need for money and the ability to earn it through hard work.
Reversed Eight
Inner dissatisfaction means that the successes of the past count for nothing.

4 **Upright Eight**
The desire for change, but uncertainty as to the correct direction to take.
Reversed Eight
The need to explore the deeper meaning of life.

5 **Upright Eight**
New experiences and new activities bring new friends and happiness.
Reversed Eight
Be careful that others do not influence personal decision.

6 **Upright Eight**
A journey which will change attitude to life.
Reversed Eight
This is not the right moment to make changes.

7 **Upright Eight**
A deeper understanding through pain and disillusion.
Reversed Eight
A lessening of emotional dependence brings serenity.

8 **Upright Eight**
A new love interest.
Reversed Eight
Emotions can become frozen if one becomes overprotective of inner self.

9 **Upright Eight**
The past is gone, and the future is rosy.
Reversed Eight
Spiritual development results from a disappointment in love.

10 **Upright Eight**
Personal success and accomplishment bring great joy.
Reversed Eight
Stop giving unwisely. Learn to say no to others.

5 Possible goal or destiny	**10** The final outcome
1	**9** Querent's hopes and ideals
4 Past influences / **2** Immediate influences / **6** Future influences	
Present position of querent	**8** Family and friends
3 Recent influences	**7** Querent's negative feelings

86

Seven of Cups

Provided the right choice is made, a dream will come true. This card also signifies mental or creative ability, mystical experiences, or an unexpected event which could bring happiness. When reversed, it means unrealistic goals, the dissipation of energies, or a lack of self-confidence.

SUGGESTED READING

1 Upright or Reversed Seven
A dream could come true if the right decision is made.

2 Upright or Reversed Seven
Mental or creative activity results in a surprising bonus.

3 Upright Seven
Too many conflicting interests; settle for one.
Reversed Seven
A difficult choice must be made. Be realistic.

4 Upright Seven
Stop daydreaming about things and get started.
Reversed Seven
Persistent work or study reaps reward.

5 Upright Seven
Initial success will evaporate unless it is quickly followed up.
Reversed Seven
Ignore opposition. Have faith in own abilities.

6 Upright Seven
Progress is slowed down by indecisiveness.
Reversed Seven
Strong will and determination will ensure success.

7 Upright Seven
Self-deception and dissipation of natural talents bring failure.
Reversed Seven
Be persistent and follow ideas through to attain success.

8 Upright Seven
An emotional choice made with honesty and a sense of realism.
Reversed Seven
Share a dream with a loved one and be guided by their good advice.

9 Upright Seven
Timidity and lack of confidence in self can undermine ambitions.
Reversed Seven
An unexpected event results in beneficial change.

10 Upright Seven
Consistent effort, self-honesty, and practical approach needed to fuel aims.
Reversed Seven
Ability, self-knowledge, and intelligent choice bring realization of a dream.

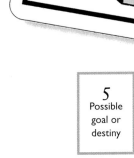
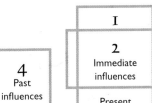

	5 Possible goal or destiny		**10** The final outcome
4 Past influences	**1** / **2** Immediate influences / Present position of querent	**6** Future influences	**9** Querent's hopes and ideals
	3 Recent influences		**8** Family and friends
			7 Querent's negative feelings

Six of Cups

This card suggests new knowledge, opportunities, and enjoyment with their roots in the past. An old friend or lover reappears, or there could be a new friendship with links to the past. When reversed, it can mean a refusal to grow up, or the need to escape a stifling situation.

SUGGESTED READING

1 Upright or Reversed Six
Past actions or influences favorably affect the present.

2 Upright or Reversed Six
Gain from the past or an imminent inheritance.

3 Upright Six
Innocent, uncritical love is given and received.
Reversed Six
The refusal to grow up causes difficulty in adapting to changing situation.

4 Upright Six
Past efforts bring present rewards.
Reversed Six
Plans could fail through inability to move forward with the times.

5 Upright Six
Old dreams are resurrected to become new goals in life.
Reversed Six
The past must be viewed realistically if future success. is to be assured.

6 Upright Six
New knowledge allied to old skills brings new opportunities and enjoyment.
Reversed Six
Delays will test courage, but are followed by success.

7 Upright Six
Old friends bring good news or gifts.
Reversed Six
A special event or journey may have to be postponed.

8 Upright Six
A new friend with much in common enters life.
Reversed Six
The need to escape a stifling relationship or situation.

9 Upright Six
A new understanding comes from testing the dreams of the past.
Reversed Six
An old conflict will be resolved shortly.

10 Upright Six
A long-held desire with roots in the past is finally realized.
Reversed Six
A slight disappointment or delay regarding financial matters or an inheritance.

	5 Possible goal or destiny	10 The final outcome
	1 2 Immediate influences Present position of querent	9 Querent's hopes and ideals
4 Past influences		6 Future influences
		8 Family and friends
	3 Recent influences	7 Querent's negative feelings

Five of Cups

The crossroads card, this denotes the end of an old life but the prospect of exciting developments in the near future. It can also signify the need for reevaluation. When reversed, the meanings are more positive: an unexpected gift; the return of an old friend; a time for healing rifts.

SUGGESTED READING

1 Upright or Reversed Five
A time of taking stock before making a major change.

2 Upright or Reversed Five
New alternatives to be evaluated and explored.

3 Upright Five
Dissatisfaction or loss brings the urge to try something new.
Reversed Five
Don't cry over spilt milk; it is in the past.

4 Upright Five
Sadness through unfulfilled expectations.
Reversed Five
Put disappointment behind and look to a new beginning.

5 Upright Five
The end of one phase of life, the start of another.
Reversed Five
A time for healing rifts and starting again.

6 Upright Five
Regret through a wrong choice or course of action.
Reversed Five
Learn from past mistakes.

7 Upright Five
The good things in life are ignored when the mind is fixed on losses.
Reversed Five
A new kind of work or a new domicile must be considered.

8 Upright Five
Friendship or romantic relationship that lacks real love is doomed to die.
Reversed Five
A happy meeting with an old friend or loved one.

9 Upright Five
Inner turmoil and lost sense of balance result from grief or disillusionment.
Reversed Five
Having the courage to face up to things realistically assures success.

10 Upright Five
A loss of some kind, but with something of value still remaining.
Reversed Five
A happy new alliance or an inheritance of some sort.

	5 Possible goal or destiny		10 The final outcome
4 Past influences	I / 2 Immediate influences / Present position of querent	6 Future influences	9 Querent's hopes and ideals
	3 Recent influences		8 Family and friends
			7 Querent's negative feelings

Four of Cups

Known as the "divine discontent," this card denotes dissatisfaction with present circumstances, which prompts the desire for a new direction. When reversed, it indicates timidity in trying something new, or unrealistic expectations leading to disappointment.

SUGGESTED READING

1 Upright or Reversed Four
The need to reevaluate past successes and achievements.

2 Upright or Reversed Four
Seeking new paths in life; moving onward.

3 Upright Four
Discontent with present circumstances brings strong desire for change.
Reversed Four
The need to recognize that anger can come from fear and insecurity.

4 Upright Four
A new approach to old problems proves: successful.
Reversed Four
Sound ideas and hard work are needed to attain success.

5 Upright Four
A positive change is on the horizon.
Reversed Four
Timidity in facing a new challenge could lead to defeat.

6 Upright Four
Make plans, look ahead; something new is in the wind.
Reversed Four
Pique or anger with others could lead to defeat.

7 Upright Four
Spiritual satisfaction from looking deeply and realistically at relationships.
Reversed Four
Outside interference can sever an emotional bond.

8 Upright Four
Kindness and help from friends and family.
Reversed Four
Unrealistic expectations in a relationship fuel previously hidden resentment.

9 Upright Four
New contacts. new relationships. or new goals.
Reversed Four
Resenting help offered could lead to lost opportunity.

10 Upright Four
Exciting events occur after a delay.
Reversed Four
A period of stagnation before a new opportunity arrives.

5 Possible goal or destiny		10 The final outcome
1		9 Querent's hopes and ideals
4 Past influences	2 Immediate influences / Present position of querent	6 Future influences / 8 Family and friends
3 Recent Influences		7 Querent's negative feelings

THE SUIT OF CUPS

Three of Cups

This card indicates emotional fulfillment, the beginning of a new phase, or latent creative talent discovered. It can also mean good fortune or victory. When reversed, it indicates overindulgence, the tendency to dwell on past misfortune, and the dissipation of energy and talents.

SUGGESTED READING

1 Upright or Reversed Three
A healing of wounds; the righting of wrongs.

2 Upright or Reversed Three
The beginning of a new chapter in life.

3 Upright Three
Exploring life's experiences more fully brings a rich reward.
Reversed Three
Flexibility and self-discipline are needed to face unwelcome changes.

4 Upright Three
Dormant talents now coming to fruition.
Reversed Three
New interests needed to widen horizons.

5 Upright Three
Learning to trust brings emotional fulfillment.
Reversed Three
Dwelling too much on the past can bring pain.

6 Upright Three
A genuine love of the community and a desire to help other people.
Reversed Three
Spiritual ties with others need to be worked through, not avoided.

7 Upright Three
A family celebration brings happiness.
Reversed Three
Overindulgence of physical appetites brings boredom and feelings of discontent.

8 Upright Three
A birth or new way of life begins.
Reversed Three
Sex without love brings loneliness and discontent.

9 Upright Three
A happy issue of an undertaking or venture.
Reversed Three
A jealous friend tries to destroy self-confidence.

10 Upright Three
Abundance of love and self-fulfillment.
Reversed Three
Self-pity is destructive and wastes time.

	5 Possible goal or destiny		**10** The final outcome
	1 / **2** Immediate influences / Present position of querent		**9** Querent's hopes and ideals
4 Past influences		**6** Future influences	**8** Family and friends
	3 Recent influences		**7** Querent's negative feelings

91

TWO of CUPS

A meeting with a like-minded person and the beginning of a friendship, partnership, or love affair are suggested by this card. It denotes the end of rivalry, or a joyous surprise. When reversed, it indicates misunderstandings, violent passions, and destructive pride.

SUGGESTED READING

1 **Upright or Reversed Two**
A meeting and emotional exchange with a kindred soul.

2 **Upright or Reversed Two**
A loving union or partnership.

3 **Upright Two**
An unexpected development changes a business or emotional partnership for the better.
Reversed Two
Quarrels are soonest resolved by using intellect rather than emotions.

4 **Upright Two**
The reconciliation of opposites clears the way for future advancement.
Reversed Two
Separation caused by a conflict of interest.

5 **Upright Two**
Signing a beneficial contract or treaty.
Reversed Two
Financial expectations are restricted or delayed.

6 **Upright Two**
A partner who will help achieve goals.
Reversed Two
Try to see the other point of view to avoid disagreement.

7 **Upright Two**
Surprising news or a gift brings joy.
Reversed Two
Always expecting perfection will destroy a relationship.

8 **Upright Two**
A deep understanding between two people.
Reversed Two
Divorce or sudden separation.

9 **Upright Two**
The gaining of emotional balance and self-sufficiency.
Reversed Two
The loss of an important friendship through overpossessive demands.

10 **Upright Two**
Great affection and understanding between two like-minded people.
Reversed Two
Inability to comprehend another's true feelings.

5
Possible goal or destiny

10
The final outcome

1

2
Immediate influences

Present position of querent

4
Past influences

6
Future influences

9
Querent's hopes and ideals

8
Family and friends

3
Recent influences

7
Querent's negative feelings

Ace of Cups

The Ace of Cups means the beginning of great joy and artistic inspiration. It also denotes home and property concerns, and if near other love cards, it indicates true love. When reversed, it means a hesitancy to nurture loving feelings; false love; and an overdeveloped ego.

SUGGESTED READING

1 Upright or Reversed Ace
Spiritual nourishment and emotional replenishment.

2 Upright or Reversed Ace
Good news coming to the home, bringing joy, happiness, and contentment.

3 Upright Ace
Creative talent and business enterprise.
Reversed Ace
Overindulgence results in inertia and lost opportunity.

4 Upright Ace
The beginning of productiveness through outpouring of love.
Reversed Ace
Unrequited affection brings loneliness and insecurity.

5 Upright Ace
A new beginning in love or a new home brings joy.
Reversed Ace
Attention to detail is required in official or legal matters.

6 Upright Ace
Satisfactory conclusion of an emotional matter.
Reversed Ace
There is a hesitancy to nurture loving feelings.

7 Upright Ace
Domestic matters enter a new phase.
Reversed Ace
Emotional imbalance results in loss.

8 Upright Ace
True love and friendship through giving and receiving in equal measures.
Reversed Ace
Over-impressed by superficial physical beauty.

9 Upright Ace
Increasing spiritual awareness brings new sense of purpose in life.
Reversed Ace
Self-centeredness can destroy a relationship.

10 Upright Ace
Great rewards from positive, loving partnership.
Reversed Ace
True love of self leads to spiritual benefits.

5 Possible goal or destiny		**10** The final outcome
1 / **2** Immediate influences / Present position of querent		**9** Querent's hopes and ideals
4 Past influences	**6** Future influences	**8** Family and friends
3 Recent influences		**7** Querent's negative feelings

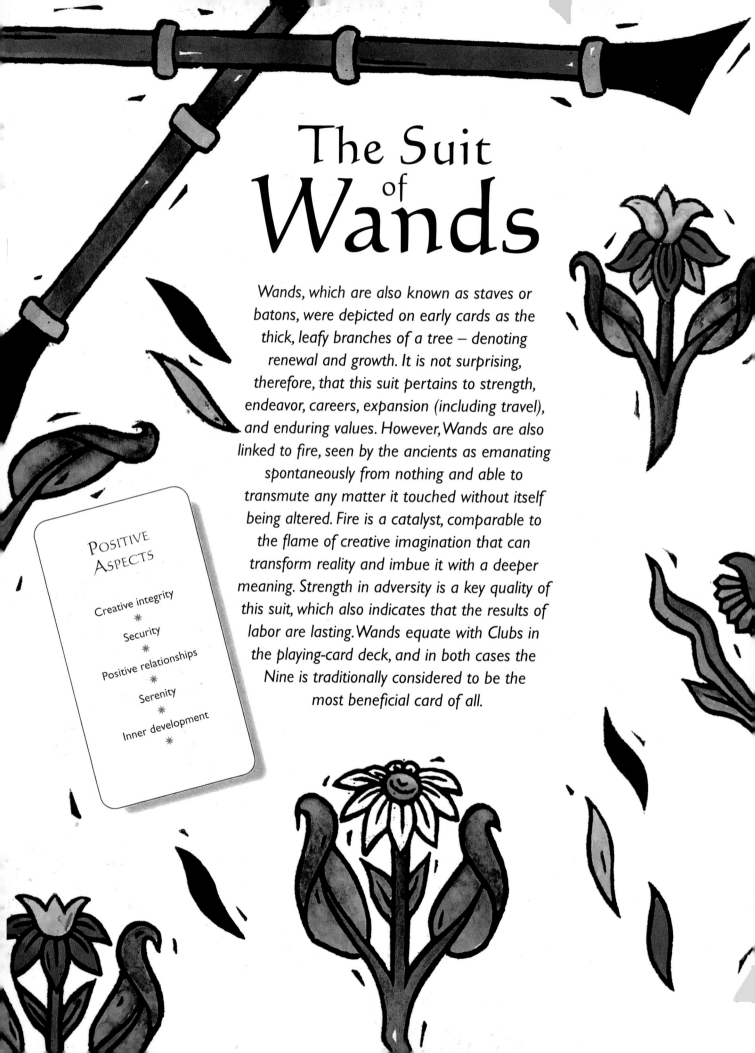

The Suit of Wands

Wands, which are also known as staves or batons, were depicted on early cards as the thick, leafy branches of a tree – denoting renewal and growth. It is not surprising, therefore, that this suit pertains to strength, endeavor, careers, expansion (including travel), and enduring values. However, Wands are also linked to fire, seen by the ancients as emanating spontaneously from nothing and able to transmute any matter it touched without itself being altered. Fire is a catalyst, comparable to the flame of creative imagination that can transform reality and imbue it with a deeper meaning. Strength in adversity is a key quality of this suit, which also indicates that the results of labor are lasting. Wands equate with Clubs in the playing-card deck, and in both cases the Nine is traditionally considered to be the most beneficial card of all.

POSITIVE ASPECTS

Creative integrity
*
Security
*
Positive relationships
*
Serenity
*
Inner development
*

NEGATIVE
ASPECTS

Disrupted work
✳
Treachery
✳
Laziness
✳
Ignorance
✳
Romantic jealousy
✳

King of WANDS

ROY · DE · BÂTON

The King of Wands is a leader with integrity and courage, a man over 35 with fiery enthusiasm, who can be successful in both creative and financial fields. A bad loser, he can be selfish and power-hungry. This card also means business success and an unexpected heritage.

SUGGESTED READING

1 Upright or Reversed King
A forceful, loyal, and conscientious leader, who can sometimes be overbearing, will open the way to unexpected business success.

2 Upright or Reversed King
Help in promotion of ideas will bring unexpected success.

3 Upright King
Sudden opportunity offered for successfully promoting new ideas.
Reversed King
Ensure all information is correct before acting.

4 Upright King
Inspirational and creative ideas will fill others with enthusiasm.
Reversed King
To be driven by the desire for power is dangerous.

5 Upright King
Leadership qualities gain recognition from others.
Reversed King
Be the first to withdraw from any argument.

6 Upright King
A strong conviction and ability to manifest new ideas.
Reversed King
Intolerance puts a strain on working relationships.

7 Upright King
Enthusiasm and clever strategy will win the day.
Reversed King
Beware of hasty judgments.

8 Upright King
The desire to improve conditions for others.
Reversed King
Material concerns can sometimes be disregarded, causing trouble to others.

9 Upright King
New ideas lead to exciting new life.
Reversed King
Admitting sometimes to being wrong is good for the soul.

10 Upright King
Successful business brings financial gain.
Reversed King
Undervaluing of the emotional needs of others can cause loss.

5 Possible goal or destiny	**10** The final outcome

1
2 Immediate influences
Present position of querent

4 Past influences

6 Future influences

3 Recent influences

9 Querent's hopes and ideals

8 Family and friends

7 Querent's negative feelings

Queen of WANDS

An intuitive, open-hearted, protective woman, the Queen of Wands is also strong-willed, confident, independent, and often gifted artistically, but she can be domineering, narrow-minded, bitter, and judgmental. This card also means success in a creative area or business.

REYNE · DE · BATON

SUGGESTED READING

I **Upright or Reversed Queen**
A generous, tolerant, friendly woman will assist or advise the querent concerning home, career, or finances.

2 **Upright or Reversed Queen**
A woman who will counsel or help in a matter connected with home or career.

3 **Upright Queen**
Patience and tolerance create favorable working and living conditions.
Reversed Queen
Being over-independent can spoil a romance.

4 **Upright Queen**
Sound business judgment brings a period of financial stability.
Reversed Queen
Stubborn refusal to admit own mistakes can damage relationships with others.

5 **Upright Queen**
Past generosity to others is repaid tenfold.
Reversed Queen
A female friend is in need of some support.

6 **Upright Queen**
Advice from capable woman ensures success.
Reversed Queen
Loved ones must be allowed their independence.

7 **Upright Queen**
Learn to trust in own intuitive feelings.
Reversed Queen
Jealousy caused by low self-esteem can damage prospects of success.

8 **Upright Queen**
A loving friend gives unselfish aid.
Reversed Queen
Learn to control emotions.

9 **Upright Queen**
Success, particularly in financial undertakings.
Reversed Queen
Have confidence; do not lose faith in own abilities.

IO **Upright Queen**
Stable home life and material comfort.
Reversed Queen
Sustain heart's goal; do not give up on oneself.

5 Possible goal or destiny	**IO** The final outcome
I / **2** Immediate influences / Present position of querent	**9** Querent's hopes and ideals
4 Past influences	**6** Future influences	**8** Family and friends
3 Recent influences	**7** Querent's negative feelings

97

Knight of WANDS

CAVALIER · DE · BATON

A lovable 21- to 35-year-old, the Knight of Wands is volatile, imaginative, and charming, and loves novelty and travel. He can mean jealousy of a lover, interference with work, or lack of energy. This card can also mean a change of residence, distant travel, or business rivalry.

SUGGESTED READING

1 Upright or Reversed Knight
An exciting young man, whose statements are to be taken with a pinch of salt, will rush into the querent's life like a breath of fresh air.

2 Upright or Reversed Knight
A sudden decision, possibly resulting in a long journey or a complete change of location.

3 Upright Knight
Intuitive feeling of a strong need for change.
Reversed Knight
There is a need to be more adventurous in life.

4 Upright Knight
Conflict and competition in career or business.
Reversed Knight
Too many irons in the fire at once. Concentrate on one idea or project.

5 Upright Knight
Trusting own inner voices brings stability.
Reversed Knight
Fear of revealing own feelings.

6 Upright Knight
A sudden decision brings some new challenges.
Reversed Knight
A legal loss caused by a careless attitude.

7 Upright Knight
Romance rushing into life, but don't be swept away.
Reversed Knight
Yearning for greener pastures brings discontent.

8 Upright Knight
A wish granted through unexpected money or legacy.
Reversed Knight
A minor dispute over or with a young person.

9 Upright Knight
Harmonious and happy domestic life.
Reversed Knight
Increased insight shows the true path to fulfillment.

10 Upright Knight
A new way of life brings both happiness and financial gain.
Reversed Knight
A long journey shows that distant fields are not always greener than those nearby.

5
Possible goal or destiny

10
The final outcome

1
2
Immediate influences
Present position of querent

9
Querent's hopes and ideals

4
Past influences

6
Future influences

8
Family and friends

3
Recent influences

7
Querent's negative feelings

Knave of WANDS

The Knave of Wands is a spiritual young person under 21, who has creative potential but has not yet chosen a direction in life. This card signifies stimulating financial news, or inspirational ideas that need nurturing. It can also mean cruelty, instability, and fear of domination.

VALET · DE · BÂTON

SUGGESTED READING

1 Upright or Reversed Knave
A well-intentioned young person brings inspiring or joyful news concerned with work, particularly that of a creative nature.

2 Upright or Reversed Knave
A message bringing joy.

3 Upright Knave
The prospect of work achieving financial gain.
Reversed Knave
Plans may be impractical and must be reassessed.

4 Upright Knave
A new stirring of creative potential.
Reversed Knave
Restlessness and inability to make the right choice.

5 Upright Knave
New methods bring sudden financial advancement.
Reversed Knave
Tendency to dominate or overrule others can destroy a partnership.

6 Upright Knave
Good news leads to prospect of advancement.
Reversed Knave
A new acquaintance brings spiritual enlightenment.

7 Upright Knave
Look inside self to gain inner security.
Reversed Knave
Lack of self-knowledge can misdirect or deceive.

8 Upright Knave
Joyful news from a friend or partner.
Reversed Knave
Bad news in the form of malicious gossip.

9 Upright Knave
Sudden financial gain.
Reversed Knave
Be aware that aims could perhaps be unrealistic.

10 Upright Knave
Sudden inspiration brings beginning of new cycle.
Reversed Knave
A sudden, unexpected meeting brings a new love.

		5 Possible goal or destiny		**10** The final outcome
		1		
4 Past influences		**2** Immediate influences	**6** Future influences	**9** Querent's hopes and ideals
		Present position of querent		**8** Family and friends
		3 Recent influences		**7** Querent's negative feelings

99

Ten of WANDS

A burden soon to be lifted is the theme of this card, but certain ideas must be relinquished before a new life begins. There may be consolidation in business, or a trip to a strange place. When reversed, risks are feared, abilities are overestimated, and deception may be used.

SUGGESTED READING

1 Upright or Reversed Ten
A long-standing problem will soon be solved.

2 Upright or Reversed Ten
The determination to see a demanding project right through to the finish.

3 Upright Ten
Relying on own strength to solve a problem.
Reversed Ten
A test or trial that refines the soul.

4 Upright Ten
A new attitude after shedding negativity.
Reversed Ten
A heart tried by pain.

5 Upright Ten
A burden soon to be lifted and happiness gained.
Reversed Ten
Power unwisely used can bring loss.

6 Upright Ten
Business consolidation brings success.
Reversed Ten
Energy applied selfishly will result in loss.

7 Upright Ten
The end of narrow-minded, fixed ideas.
Reversed Ten
The refusal to take a risk slows progress.

8 Upright Ten
A reunion with loved one or family at a distance.
Reversed Ten
Excessive pressure and strain can damage relationships.

9 Upright Ten
A difficult time is now coming to an end.
Reversed Ten
Weighed down by false values and needless worry.

10 Upright Ten
A goal is reached and life is transformed.
Reversed Ten
Progress impeded by refusal to shed old prejudices.

5
Possible goal or destiny

10
The final outcome

1
2
Immediate influences
Present position of querent

9
Querent's hopes and ideals

4
Past influences

6
Future influences

8
Family and friends

3
Recent influences

7
Querent's negative feelings

Nine of WANDS

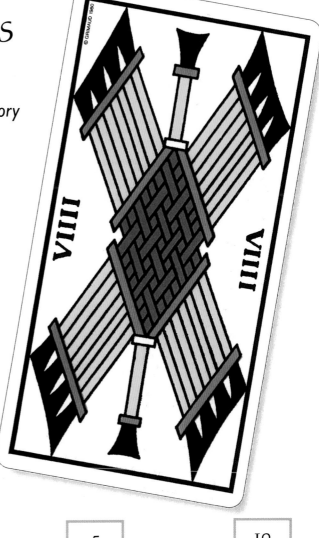

This is the strongest card of the minor arcana, representing triumph after a final challenge, and victory through strength and integrity. When reversed, it indicates too great a trust in others, difficulty in accepting delay, and lack of initiative.

SUGGESTED READING

I **Upright or Reversed Nine**
A safe and assured position. Intuitively knows the right way. Takes responsibility for own actions and is not afraid to fight for own rights and those of others.

2 **Upright or Reversed Nine**
A challenge fought which results in triumph.

3 **Upright Nine**
A stable position will be gained after a struggle.
Reversed Nine
Self-protection must be maintained to avoid hurt.

4 **Upright Nine**
Intuitive awareness of reactions of others ensures smooth progress.
Reversed Nine
Discretion must be used when discussing new ideas or issues with others.

5 **Upright Nine**
Steady, slow, sure progress brings lasting benefit.
Reversed Nine
Advice from authority must not be disregarded.

6 **Upright Nine**
Struggles and pressure of work are inevitable.
Reversed Nine
Narrow views and fixed ideas can hinder progress.

7 **Upright Nine**
Strength in reserve and courage against all odds ensure victory.
Reversed Nine
It is important not to ignore health matters.

8 **Upright Nine**
Encouragement and help from a friend.
Reversed Nine
Hidden hostility from others is suddenly revealed.

9 **Upright Nine**
One last battle before the war is won.
Reversed Nine
Keep heart high for one last try to achieve your goal.

IO **Upright Nine**
Victory through strength and integrity.
Reversed Nine
A delayed triumph.

	5 Possible goal or destiny		**IO** The final outcome
	I / **2** Immediate influences / Present position of querent		**9** Querent's hopes and ideals
4 Past influences		**6** Future influences	**8** Family and friends
	3 Recent influences		**7** Querent's negative feelings

Eight of WANDS

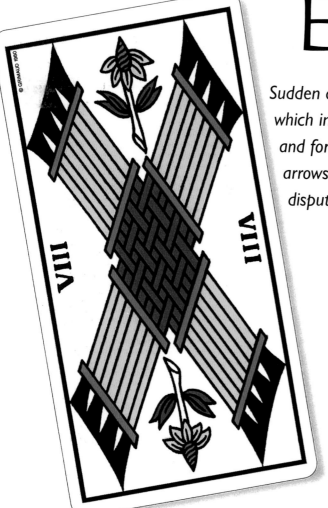

Sudden change and progress are the keynotes of this card, which indicates the end of a delay, unexpected news, and foreign travel, especially by air. It can also mean the arrows of love. When reversed, it can denote sudden disputes, jealousy, insecurity, and thoughtless action.

SUGGESTED READING

1 Upright or Reversed Eight
A time for taking the initiative.

2 Upright or Reversed Eight
Exciting news shatters period of calm or stagnation.

3 Upright Eight
Aiming for change and a new goal in life.
Reversed Eight
New creative energies must be used wisely.

4 Upright Eight
Delay or pause after active struggle.
Reversed Eight
Decisions made too hastily.

5 Upright Eight
Swift action brings positive results.
Reversed Eight
Sudden thoughtless action brings problems.

6 Upright Eight
A new idea needs a quick decision to be made.
Reversed Eight
To overcome a misunderstanding, swift communication is needed.

7 Upright Eight
A challenge will be quickly overcome.
Reversed Eight
Hidden enemies speedily revealed and vanquished.

8 Upright Eight
Love comes suddenly.
Reversed Eight
Jealousy spoils prospects in romantic relationship.

9 Upright Eight
Swift progress made in new undertaking.
Reversed Eight
Flight to overseas, or overseas connection in business.

10 Upright Eight
There will be success in a new venture.
Reversed Eight
Sudden disputes cause delays.

5
Possible goal or destiny

10
The final outcome

1

2
Immediate influences

Present position of querent

4
Past influences

6
Future influences

9
Querent's hopes and ideals

3
Recent influences

8
Family and friends

7
Querent's negative feelings

Seven of WANDS

The teacher card, this signifies the dissemination of knowledge through writing and teaching. It can suggest a successful change in profession and inner strength. When reversed, it can mean envy from others, the need for competitiveness, and indecision that could bring failure.

SUGGESTED READING

1 Upright or Reversed Seven
A successful change in work or profession.

2 Upright or Reversed Seven
Success will come, but only after a hard struggle.

3 Upright Seven
Abilities have been developed through sustained effort and sacrifice.
Reversed Seven
More self-confidence needed in order to utilize talents fully.

4 Upright Seven
Slow but sure progress.
Reversed Seven
Envy and opposition only strengthen determination.

5 Upright Seven
The last major challenge is now overcome.
Reversed Seven
Difficulties must be regarded positively as steps in a ladder.

6 Upright Seven
Faith in own abilities brings reward.
Reversed Seven
Competition causes needless fear and anxiety.

7 Upright Seven
Learn to value own talents and ambitions.
Reversed Seven
Hesitancy and indecision can cause loss or failure.

8 Upright Seven
Support is given for new work or change of life at a crucial time.
Reversed Seven
A test of faith is coming. Do not give up.

9 Upright Seven
Courage and spiritual strength given for successful change of direction.
Reversed Seven
Fight negativity of those around you who fear change.

10 Upright Seven
Surmounting overwhelming odds to reap success and reward.
Reversed Seven
Delays could occur through attempting too much at once.

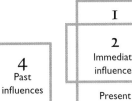

	5 Possible goal or destiny		**10** The final outcome
4 Past influences	**1** / **2** Immediate influences / Present position of querent	**6** Future influences	**9** Querent's hopes and ideals
	3 Recent influences		**8** Family and friends
			7 Querent's negative feelings

Six of WANDS

This card is one of triumph, and when reversed is only mildly negative. It indicates a victory after a struggle, public acclaim, promotion, and wonderful news. When reversed, it suggests that false pride could be an obstacle and that envy from others could sour a triumph.

SUGGESTED READING

1 Upright or Reversed Six
Success after a struggle.

2 Upright or Reversed Six
Good news brings advancement.

3 Upright Six
Hard work and effort, or creative inspiration.
Reversed Six
Need unification of energies to synthesize efforts.

4 Upright Six
Satisfaction of personal effort and hard work.
Reversed Six
Overcoming difficult trials and opposition from others.

5 Upright Six
Reward after a period of disappointment and struggle.
Reversed Six
Delayed but eventual reward.

6 Upright Six
Diplomacy overcomes opposition from others.
Reversed Six
An oppressive attitude brings a victory but no real gain.

7 Upright Six
A difficult situation will soon be resolved.
Reversed Six
Disloyalty from others can cause disappointment

8 Upright Six
A valuable ally will give his or her support.
Reversed Six
Beware that success can foster envy in others.

9 Upright Six
Success assured through intelligent and diplomatic handling of others.
Reversed Six
False pride and arrogance can often ignore the abilities of others.

10 Upright Six
Triumph after many trials and tribulations.
Reversed Six
Eventual triumph after the routing of enemies.

5
Possible goal or destiny

10
The final outcome

1

2
Immediate influences

Present position of querent

6
Future influences

9
Querent's hopes and ideals

4
Past influences

8
Family and friends

3
Recent influences

7
Querent's negative feelings

Five of WANDS

Great obstacles are indicated by this card, which can mean a struggle with material adversity. It can also signify that love can bring a triumph. When reversed, it suggests that care is needed with contracts and agreements, and that unfulfilled desires could cause embitterment.

SUGGESTED READING

1 Upright or Reversed Five
A struggle to achieve a personal ambition.

2 Upright or Reversed Five
Obstacles to be overcome.

3 Upright Five
A bold fighter; the victor of many battles.
Reversed Five
Discontent can arise from unreal expectation.

4 Upright Five
A struggle with material adversity and obstacles.
Reversed Five
Inability to compromise results in unsatisfied desires.

5 Upright Five
Victory after surmounting obstacles.
Reversed Five
Competition and possible deception from others.

6 Upright Five
New business opportunity or creative opening offered.
Reversed Five
Perception of future prospects clouded by feeling of insecurity.

7 Upright Five
Love triumphs over difficult obstacles.
Reversed Five
Rash decision based on emotion can lead to failure.

8 Upright Five
Temporary misunderstanding brings sorrow and conflict.
Reversed Five
Be aware of manipulation by those who are weaker.

9 Upright Five
A change for the better.
Reversed Five
Enforced restriction delays realization of ambition.

10 Upright Five
Success won through courage and tenacity.
Reversed Five
Compromises must be made before happiness is won.

	5 Possible goal or destiny	**10** The final outcome
	1	**9** Querent's hopes and ideals
4 Past influences	**2** Immediate influences / Present position of querent	**6** Future influences
		8 Family and friends
	3 Recent influences	**7** Querent's negative feelings

Four of WANDS

The card of the gifted inventor, the Four of Wands also signifies romance, harmony, and tranquillity, and the harvest after long labor. Its reverse is only mildly negative, indicating achievement delayed, unfulfilled romantic dreams, and the need to guard finances.

SUGGESTED READING

1 Upright or Reversed Four
A creative achievement.

2 Upright or Reversed Four
Something completed brings happiness and reward.

3 Upright Four
Consistent effort bringing satisfaction and reward.
Reversed Four
Fear of insecurity undermines confidence in self.

4 Upright Four
A new level of consciousness brings desire to achieve or create.
Reversed Four
Overmaterialistic outlook can smother creativity.

5 Upright Four
A creative idea or project is successful.
Reversed Four
An unrealistic attitude to life which restricts creativity.

6 Upright Four
Self-belief and positive action bring prosperity.
Reversed Four
A new romantic attachment brings happiness.

7 Upright Four
A welcome peaceful pause in activity.
Reversed Four
Unfulfilled romantic yearnings.

8 Upright Four
Loving friends give needed support.
Reversed Four
Snobbishness and feelings of superiority can repel others.

9 Upright Four
Rest and peace after a period of hard work.
Reversed Four
Further effort needed to attain goal.

10 Upright Four
Perfected work brings future success.
Reversed Four
Take care that work is not hidebound by convention.

---

5 Possible goal or destiny

10 The final outcome

1 Immediate influences

2 Present position of querent

4 Past influences

6 Future influences

9 Querent's hopes and ideals

8 Family and friends

3 Recent influences

7 Querent's negative feelings

106

Three of WANDS

Powerful convictions, originality, and talent are the domain of this card. It means the start of a promising enterprise, and can denote inspirational work bringing recognition and reward. When it is reversed, inability to adapt can inhibit progress and careless methods can bring failure.

SUGGESTED READING

1 Upright or Reversed Three
A partnership brings wealth and fame.

2 Upright or Reversed Three
An offer of help or partnership in new project or idea, which must be acted on immediately.

3 Upright Three
Good foundation laid for successful enterprise.
Reversed Three
Consultation with established person or authority helps accomplish aims.

4 Upright Three
Practical matters need security and efficient handling.
Reversed Three
Opportunity lost if slipshod methods used.

5 Upright Three
Successful completion of initial phase of commercial or artistic project.
Reversed Three
Failure to give ideas a means of practical expression.

6 Upright Three
Work that challenges and requires mental effort.
Reversed Three
Caution against arrogance in business dealings.

7 Upright Three
Assistance from expert demands self-honesty.
Reversed Three
Beware of assistance offered for the wrong motives.

8 Upright Three
Powerful man of inspirational turn of mind gives valuable support.
Reversed Three
Loss could occur through inability to change ideas.

9 Upright Three
New plans put into action bring reward.
Reversed Three
Alteration causes disappointment but the resulting delay is fortunate.

10 Upright Three
Artist or inventor turns dreams into reality, or a new business project is launched successfully.
Reversed Three
Envy of others could mar sense of achievement.

5 Possible goal or destiny	**10** The final outcome

4 Past influences	**1** / **2** Immediate influences / Present position of querent	**6** Future influences	**9** Querent's hopes and ideals

8 Family and friends

3 Recent Influences

7 Querent's negative feelings

Two of WANDS

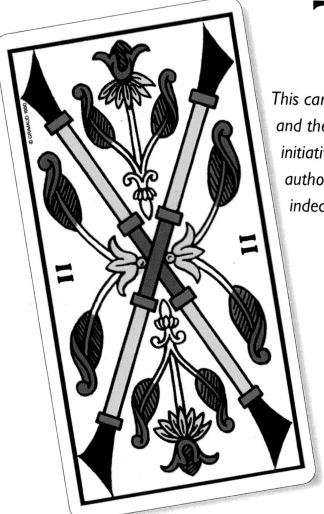

This card indicates attainment through steady application, and the achievement of maturity through courage and initiative. It suggests that strength and vision result in authority and success. When reversed, it can mean indecisiveness, restlessness, and obstinacy.

SUGGESTED READING

1 Upright or Reversed Two
Success through strength and clear vision.

2 Upright or Reversed Two
Influential person or authority gives generous help.

3 Upright Two
Progress has solid base of research, learning, and consistent application.
Reversed Two
Foundations laid may not bring desired result.

4 Upright Two
Strength and vision will bring favorable results.
Reversed Two
Criticism from others must be dealt with wisely.

5 Upright Two
Help given for new idea brings success.
Reversed Two
Right choices must be made to ensure stable progress.

6 Upright Two
Act on own intuition and success is certain.
Reversed Two
Loss of faith in future project caused by envy and criticism.

7 Upright Two
It is harder to be a gracious receiver than a generous giver.
Reversed Two
A proud and unforgiving nature often chooses the wrong road in life.

8 Upright Two
Strength of will and ambition bring fulfillment.
Reversed Two
Success proves to be worthless when love is smothered by ambition.

9 Upright Two
Strength, initiative. and vision ensure future success.
Reversed Two
Overemphasis on material security can prohibit risk and prevent attainment.

10 Upright Two
With help, a situation is mastered and a goal is reached.
Reversed Two
Imposed restraint must be endured with patience in order to succeed.

```
        ┌──────────┐        ┌──────────┐
        │    5     │        │   IO     │
        │ Possible │        │The final │
        │ goal or  │        │ outcome  │
        │ destiny  │        │          │
        └──────────┘        └──────────┘

┌──────┐ ┌──────────┐ ┌──────┐   ┌──────────┐
│      │ │    I     │ │      │   │    9     │
│  4   │ │    2     │ │  6   │   │ Querent's│
│ Past │ │Immediate │ │Future│   │  hopes   │
│influ-│ │influences│ │influ-│   │and ideals│
│ences │ │          │ │ences │   └──────────┘
│      │ │ Present  │ │      │   ┌──────────┐
│      │ │ position │ │      │   │    8     │
│      │ │of querent│ │      │   │  Family  │
└──────┘ └──────────┘ └──────┘   │   and    │
                                 │ friends  │
        ┌──────────┐             └──────────┘
        │    3     │             ┌──────────┐
        │  Recent  │             │    7     │
        │influences│             │ Querent's│
        └──────────┘             │ negative │
                                 │ feelings │
                                 └──────────┘
```

Ace of WANDS

Renewal is the theme of this card. It can mean a new beginning; an up rush of creative energy or vision; dissatisfaction that heralds a change; the founding of a fortune; or an inheritance. When reversed, it denotes a false start or goals unrealized because of restlessness.

SUGGESTED READING

1 Upright or Reversed Ace
Dissatisfaction with present life breeds a restlessness that leads to change.

2 Upright or Reversed Ace
A new enterprise or new phase in life.

3 Upright Ace
Having a second look at prospective goal in life.
Reversed Ace
Unformulated goals which need defining.

4 Upright Ace
Uprush of creative fire and energy.
Reversed Ace
The beginning of a new spiritual understanding.

5 Upright Ace
An original concept which will succeed.
Reversed Ace
Basis of family fortune will be created.

6 Upright Ace
Clear thinking needed if aims are to succeed.
Reversed Ace
Delays postpone completion of project.

7 Upright Ace
Dramatic insights bring a new way of thinking.
Reversed Ace
An effort must be made to break an old pattern or habits.

8 Upright Ace
Some unexpected money or an inheritance.
Reversed Ace
Spiritual emptiness and lack of spiritual growth.

9 Upright Ace
A new awareness of the spiritual aspect of life changes goals in life.
Reversed Ace
Unrealized ambition brings feelings of dissatisfaction.

10 Upright Ace
A new creation, a new life, a new goal, or a new adventure. An empty existence is transformed.
Reversed Ace
A new beginning after delay. A disputed inheritance or gift of money will eventuate.

5 Possible goal or destiny			**10** The final outcome
	1 **2** Immediate influences Present position of querent	**6** Future influences	**9** Querent's hopes and ideals
4 Past influences			**8** Family and friends
	3 Recent influences		**7** Querent's negative feelings

The Suit of Pentacles

The Pentacle is represented by a gold coin showing the five-pointed star of Hermes, the god of alchemy and commerce, and finance dominates this suit. Pentacles correspond with the earth, the provider of nourishment, shelter, clothing, and work whose reward conveys a sense of worth. The suit of Pentacles describes the material world, with its everyday struggles, the value placed on a person's achievements, losses and gains in commercial transactions, and the risks associated with financial ventures, which can involve litigation. The corresponding suit in playing cards is Diamonds, which is equally connected with affluence and influence. The suit of Pentacles also contains a warning that money can be the root of all evil, and that its, misuse – through too strong an attachment to it, or too great a fear or contempt of it – can result in suffering and extreme poverty of the spirit.

POSITIVE ASPECTS

Generosity

*

Financial reward

*

Stability

*

Success at work

*

Craftsmanship

*

NEGATIVE
ASPECTS

Meanness
*
Covetousness
*
Poverty
*
Unemployment
*
Isolation
*

King of PENTACLES

Often associated with financial matters, the King of Pentacles is a patient, intuitive, inarticulate, and loyal man of over 35, with mathematical ability. Stable and cautious, he is protective of his friends. But he could be thriftless, easy to bribe, shallow, and opinionated.

ROY · DE · DENIERS

SUGGESTED READING

1 **Upright or Reversed King**
A patient man of high position may bring friendship, assistance, or advice.

2 **Upright or Reversed King**
Ideals have served the querent well, but now it is time to concentrate on the material aspect of life.

3 **Upright King**
Financial stability achieved through cautious progress.
Reversed King
Greed is seldom allied to caution and sound judgment.

4 **Upright King**
Professional advice puts affairs on a sound footing.
Reversed King.
Ensure that correct business methods are employed.

5 **Upright King**
A financial goal is reached after a struggle.
Reversed King
Refuse to be intimidated by others, or coerced into taking the wrong action.

6 **Upright King**
The unexpected discovery of an aptitude for financial management.
Reversed King
A talent for finance, if misused, can lead to trouble.

7 **Upright King**
An upturn in business, or a promotion, brings financial increase.
Reversed King
Make sure that a business associate is trustworthy.

8 **Upright King**
A powerful new friend will advise and protect.
Reversed King
Take care that the time is right for financial speculation.

9 **Upright King**
Self-confidence boosted by material success.
Reversed King
Do not be carried away by success. Keep feet firmly on the ground.

10 **Upright King**
Money made from own efforts brings fulfillment.
Reversed King
Preoccupation with business affairs can lead to neglect of loved ones.

5 Possible goal or destiny		**10** The final outcome
	1	**9** Querent's hopes and ideals
4 Past influences	**2** Immediate influences	**6** Future influences
	Present position of querent	**8** Family and friends
3 Recent influences		**7** Querent's negative feelings

Queen of PENTACLES

A woman, possibly of independent means, practical, materialistic, interested in the arts, and socially oriented, the Queen of Pentacles is a hard worker, who is self-reliant and gives to those who interest her. She can be insecure, untrusting, and overinfluenced by the physical.

SUGGESTED READING

I Upright or Reversed Queen
A self-sufficient, financially oriented woman may give friendship or advice. This card also means money-making, and responsibility to society.

2 Upright or Reversed Queen
A gifted, practical woman who will influence the querent's life.

3 Upright Queen
The opportunity to utilize talents to create a secure environment.
Reversed Queen
Beware of dwelling on past successes, which can create a false sense of security.

4 Upright Queen
Personal satisfaction attained from help given to others less fortunate.
Reversed Queen
Be wary of help given by manipulative woman.

5 Upright Queen
An interest in the arts or civic affairs brings satisfaction.
Reversed Queen
Problems could arise from neglect of financial affairs.

6 Upright Queen
Good use of practical talents ensures prosperity.
Reversed Queen
An unnecessary fear of failure could impede progress.

7 Upright Queen
The need to recognize that physical pleasures enrich and preserve life.
Reversed Queen
Melancholy can come from a sense of isolation.

8 Upright Queen
Inner strength earns the respect of loved ones.
Reversed Queen
Underestimation of own abilities can result in dependence on others.

9 Upright Queen
The good use of own abilities brings harmony.
Reversed Queen
Business responsibilities could be neglected through a feeling of insecurity and isolation.

IO Upright Queen
Financial acumen, hard work, and ability create a lasting achievement.
Reversed Queen
A present need to husband both energy and finances.

5 Possible goal or destiny		**IO** The final outcome
I **2** Immediate influences Present position of querent		**9** Querent's hopes and ideals
4 Past influences	**6** Future influences	**8** Family and friends
3 Recent influences		**7** Querent's negative feelings

Knight of PENTACLES

CAVALIER·DE·DENIERS

An upright, honorable, persevering young man, the Knight of Pentacles loves nature and animals. He is also materialistic and can be mean. Timid and insecure, he can make mistakes though lack of confidence, and waste his talents. He can also denote stagnation.

SUGGESTED READING

1 Upright or Reversed Knight
A persistent, traditional, and responsible young man. Can also mean laborious work, yielding substantial reward, or a sexual indiscretion.

2 Upright or Reversed Knight
A young man bringing encouragement and friendship to the querent.

3 Upright Knight
Life has been hard but the future looks promising.
Reversed Knight
Mistakes could be made through timidity and shyness.

4 Upright Knight
Perseverance coupled with a responsible attitude ensures work well done.
Reversed Knight
Progress may be impeded by irresponsibility and lack of patience.

5 Upright Knight
A difficult matter seen through to the end brings unexpected reward.
Reversed Knight
Idleness can cause stagnation in business affairs.

6 Upright Knight
A methodical approach produces excellent results.
Reversed Knight
Check all aspects of a new project; do not be careless.

7 Upright Knight
Constant motivation is needed to develop talents.
Reversed Knight
An affair could wound another and damage self-respect.

8 Upright Knight
A new love brings security and ambition.
Reversed Knight
Inner dissatisfaction brings the urge to start anew.

9 Upright Knight
A lover of animals and nature, who could become a successful healer.
Reversed Knight
An empathy with those less fortunate becomes a constant drain on finances.

10 Upright Knight
Work requiring patience and concentration brings financial reward.
Reversed Knight
Dogmatic opinions and a limited viewpoint can block future progress.

5 Possible goal or destiny		10 The final outcome
1		9 Querent's hopes and ideals
4 Past influences	2 Immediate influences / Present position of querent	6 Future influences
		8 Family and friends
3 Recent influences		7 Querent's negative feelings

Knave of PENTACLES

The Knave of Pentacles represents a person under 21 who is determined, articulate, and respects education and new ideas. This card can mean a letter containing good fortune, but can also signify dissipation of talents, unreal goals, intellectual conceit, and loss of worldly goods.

VALET·DE·DENIERS

SUGGESTED READING

1 **Upright or Reversed Knave**

A young person with a thirst for knowledge, who can be materialistic, opinionated, rebellious, and sometimes illogical. Can also mean significant news or a letter containing a moderate sum.

2 **Upright or Reversed Knave**

News arriving that will bring beneficial change.

3 **Upright Knave**
High ideals, ambition, and new ideas promise success.
Reversed Knave
A love of luxury can lead to excess and loss.

4 **Upright Knave**
Physical activities or development could result in a new occupation.
Reversed Knave
Those in love with themselves seldom have any rivals.

5 **Upright Knave**
Those demanding the best in life sometimes must settle for less.
Reversed Knave
Ignoring the obvious often leads to unrealistic and unattainable expectations.

6 **Upright Knave**
A welcome letter containing money.
Reversed Knave
Small sums are better saved than squandered.

7 **Upright Knave**
Diligence, perseverance, and learning will bring slow but sure progress.
Reversed Knave
The opinions of others can often be instructive; if you listen, you learn.

8 **Upright Knave**
A new friend offers a challenging opportunity.
Reversed Knave
The lack of appreciation from loved ones could stem from own selfishness.

9 **Upright Knave**
Success will come, slowly but surely.
Reversed Knave
Rebellion is childish. Grow up and accept defeat gracefully.

10 **Upright Knave**
News coming that creates a brighter future.
Reversed Knave
Time and care are needed to develop full potential.

5 Possible goal or destiny	**10** The final outcome
1	**9** Querent's hopes and ideals
2 Immediate influences	
4 Past influences	Present position of querent	**6** Future influences	**8** Family and friends
3 Recent influences	**7** Querent's negative feelings

115

Ten of PENTACLES

This is the card of both inner and outer wealth shared with others. It can refer to property, creative achievement, the establishing of a family tradition, or an inheritance. When reversed, it can mean the burden of restrictive family ties, financial problems, and family differences.

SUGGESTED READING

1 Upright or Reversed Ten
The ability to nurture, help, and protect which comes from inner spiritual strength.

2 Upright or Reversed Ten
Recognition for past efforts.

3 Upright Ten
Security built on firm, solid foundations.
Reversed Knave
Hard work and consistent effort will bring both rewards and recognition.

4 Upright Ten
Money wisely spent ensures security.
Reversed Ten
Lack of motivation brings a number of problems.

5 Upright Ten
A happy, settled, secure way of life.
Reversed Ten
Selfish spending causes financial shortage in the home.

6 Upright Ten
The solving of a difficult financial problem.
Reversed Ten
Take care that new financial proposal is all that it seems.

7 Upright Ten
An unexpected legacy or gift brings joy.
Reversed Ten
Reverence for tradition can prevent the discarding of outworn precepts.

8 Upright Ten
Try to be objective; do not credit others with own inner strength.
Reversed Ten
The need to take command and heal a family rift.

9 Upright Ten
Plan for the future to prevent older people from being a drain on finances.
Reversed Ten
Problems with sums of money, such as wills, wages, or pensions.

10 Upright Ten
A creative project or business established will benefit others in the future.
Reversed Ten
Make sure that home and possessions are well protected and insured.

5 Possible goal or destiny

10 The final outcome

1 Immediate influences

2 Present position of querent

9 Querent's hopes and ideals

4 Past influences

6 Future influences

8 Family and friends

3 Recent influences

7 Querent's negative feelings

Nine of PENTACLES

An independent person who takes pride in unique abilities, but is still seeking personal satisfaction is indicated by this card. It can also mean the solution to a problem, often bringing material comfort. Reversed, it can imply a canceled project, a need for caution, and loneliness.

SUGGESTED READING

1 Upright or Reversed Nine
A strong sense of identity and a pride in own achievements.

2 Upright or Reversed Nine
The sudden welcome solution to a problem.

3 Upright Nine
Justified pleasure in one's own achievements.
Reversed Nine
Difficult entanglement could bring emotional loss.

4 Upright Nine
Accomplishment on the material plane.
Reversed Nine
Loneliness and boredom often result in unwise alliances.

5 Upright Nine
Large income through unexpected opportunity.
Reversed Nine
Prudence is needed to ensure financial success.

6 Upright Nine
The feeling of being incomplete leads to seeking new challenges.
Reversed Nine
Have the courage to face facts and analyze the situation.

7 Upright Nine
A self-acceptance which does not depend on the approval of others.
Reversed Nine
Use caution when entering into new relationships. Someone is strongly attracted by worldly wealth.

8 Upright Nine
Home life and nature bring great joy.
Reversed Nine
Avoid the intrigues of meddlesome people.

9 Upright Nine
Sound administration and sustained effort result in a successful outcome.
Reversed Nine
Learn to admit that being independent does not preclude needing others.

10 Upright Nine
Successful completion of a plan brings reward and comfort.
Reversed Nine
Independence is fine but learn to be a graceful receiver.

	5 Possible goal or destiny		10 The final outcome
4 Past influences	1 / 2 Immediate influences / Present position of querent	6 Future influences	9 Querent's hopes and ideals
			8 Family and friends
	3 Recent influences		7 Querent's negative feelings

117

Eight of PENTACLES

This card expresses the combination of talent and energy. The talent may only recently have been discovered, and can be turned into a rewarding profession, even in later life. When reversed, it can mean vanity, lack of concentrated effort, limited ambitions, and cunning.

SUGGESTED READING

1 Upright or Reversed Eight
Talent allied with energy brings a profitable, rewarding change of direction.

2 Upright or Reversed Eight
Employing newly discovered skills in the future.

3 Upright Eight
New talents are discovered and developed.
Reversed Eight
Hard work and small rewards lead to fully developed skills.

4 Upright Eight
Study and natural ability provide pleasing results.
Reversed Eight
An inflated ego hinders the learning process.

5 Upright Eight
The beginning of profitable, skilled, or creative work venture.
Reversed Eight
The creative urge needs consistent, sustained effort, not merely inspiration.

6 Upright Eight
A successful change of direction in career.
Reversed Eight
A sense of false security results from overestimation of own talents.

7 Upright Eight
Persevere. The goal may seem far off but it will be reached in the end.
Reversed Eight
Guidance is needed to prevent wrong attitude or methods in developing skills.

8 Upright Eight
A new interest, later in life, will bring reward.
Reversed Eight
Too self-limiting and timid to attempt something new.

9 Upright Eight
Talent and training will provide satisfying work.
Reversed Eight
Commercialism and lack of effort result in the mediocre.

10 Upright Eight
Perfected skills bring prestige and profit.
Reversed Eight
There are no shortcuts to reaching a professional standard; effort is needed.

5 Possible goal or destiny	**10** The final outcome
1 **2** Immediate influences Present position of querent	**9** Querent's hopes and ideals
4 Past influences	**6** Future influences
3 Recent influences	**8** Family and friends
	7 Querent's negative feelings

Seven of PENTACLES

A warning not to rest on past laurels is contained in this card. Continued, consistent work will bring previous efforts to fruition. The Seven of Pentacles also suggests a cycle of change. When reversed, it can indicate self-pity, anxiety, and seemingly insuperable obstacles.

SUGGESTED READING

1 Upright or Reversed Seven
Unwavering, continued effort is needed to make past efforts successful.

2 Upright or Reversed Seven
Progress after a long period of hard work.

3 Upright Seven
A pause during the development of a project.
Reversed Seven
Depression and anxiety caused by financial state.

4 Upright Seven
Patience while awaiting results of past labor.
Reversed Seven
Fear of falling can prevent exploration of new territory.

5 Upright Seven
Growth through effort and commitment.
Reversed Seven
Success will slip away without consistent endeavor.

6 Upright Seven
A sudden, unexpected gain or gift of money.
Reversed Seven
Care needed to make a difficult work decision.

7 Upright Seven
The beginning of a cycle of change that will eventually improve income.
Reversed Seven
Do not be anxious if things come to a standstill. Plan the next move and wait.

8 Upright Seven
A potential suitor with possible past connections.
Reversed Seven
Apparently insurmountable obstacles are only temporary.

9 Upright Seven
A major decision is transformed by a sudden uplift in finances.
Reversed Seven
Anxiety over money which eventuates after delay.

10 Upright Seven
Results from the past now bear fruit.
Reversed Seven
Decision whether to continue with past work or commence new project.

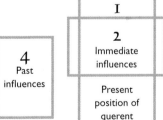

5 Possible goal or destiny		**10** The final outcome
1 / **2** Immediate influences / Present position of querent		**9** Querent's hopes and ideals
4 Past influences	**6** Future influences	**8** Family and friends
3 Recent influences		**7** Querent's negative feelings

Six of PENTACLES

The theatrical card of the minor arcana, the Six of Pentacles signifies work in front of the public, and the external manifestation of spiritual power, love, and joy. When reversed, it can imply debts, the inability to give of oneself, and insecurity over lack of recognition.

SUGGESTED READING

1 **Upright or Reversed Six**
Success and transformation.

2 **Upright or Reversed Six**
Faith is restored in life or own talents and capabilities.

3 **Upright Six**
Just rewards bring joy, wealth, and satisfaction.
Reversed Six
Friends and family return long-forgotten favors.

4 **Upright Six**
Financial affairs are put on a stable footing.
Reversed Six
Loans or unpaid bills must not be forgotten.

5 **Upright Six**
Enjoying the fruits of one's own labor.
Reversed Six
Insecurity caused by lack of recognition from others for own hard work.

6 **Upright Six**
Promotion or financial bonus in the offing.
Reversed Six
Unsatisfactory distribution of money, estate, or business.

7 **Upright Six**
A generous offer of financial help.
Reversed Six
Lawsuit over money.

8 **Upright Six**
The joy of being able to help loved ones.
Reversed Six
Envy from others causes distress and unhappiness.

9 **Upright Six**
Promotion, bonus, or profits shared with others.
Reversed Six
A financial sacrifice is repaid in a wonderful way.

10 **Upright Six**
What has been given will be returned threefold.
Reversed Six
It is easier to give money to others than to give self.

5 Possible goal or destiny	**10** The final outcome
1 **2** Immediate influences / Present position of querent	**9** Querent's hopes and ideals
4 Past influences / **6** Future influences	**8** Family and friends
3 Recent influences	**7** Querent's negative feelings

120

Five of PENTACLES

Trouble through the head being ruled by the heart is the theme of this card, which can mean loss of work, home, or position in life, but also new friends found through suffering similar hardship. When reversed, it can indicate making a new start and regaining faith in oneself.

SUGGESTED READING

1 Upright or Reversed Five
Loss and hardship result in a spiritual awakening.

2 Upright or Reversed Five
Overcoming hardship slowly but surely.

3 Upright Five
Material loss, and/or emotional loss.
Reversed Five
A strong need to make a new start in life.

4 Upright Five
Self-pride could block acceptance of help.
Reversed Five
Loss of love or security brings sense of loneliness.

5 Upright Five
Assessment of present circumstances leads to accepting a new challenge.
Reversed Five
Financial hardship is relieved.

6 Upright Five
New employment, possibly casual, points to new course of action.
Reversed Five
A legal settlement could entail a loss.

7 Upright Five
Sorrow through head being ruled by heart.
Reversed Five
Love gone astray.

8 Upright Five
An affinity with another who shares similar troubles.
Reversed Five
Failure to communicate with others through lack of empathy.

9 Upright Five
Review the past objectively and decide what is really important to achieve future happiness.
Reversed Five
Accept the lesson learned and be ready to move ahead.

10 Upright Five
Financial losses regained after hard work.
Reversed Five
Inner reorientation and wise management of finances bring eventual happiness.

		5 Possible goal or destiny	**10** The final outcome
	1 / **2** Immediate influences / Present position of querent		**9** Querent's hopes and ideals
4 Past influences		**6** Future influences	**8** Family and friends
	3 Recent influences		**7** Querent's negative feelings

121

Four of PENTACLES

Material considerations dominate this card, which can mean the establishment of a business, love of possessions, worldly gain, a legacy, and the desire for power. When reversed, it can signify miserly tendencies, obstacles in business, financial problems, and low self-valuation.

SUGGESTED READING

1 Upright or Reversed Four
Sound ability and effort result in material wealth.

2 Upright or Reversed Four
Assured financial gain.

3 Upright Four
A new commercial venture, proposition, or business position.
Reversed Four
The fear of loss results in no loss but also no gain.

4 Upright Four
The ability to work hard ensures reward.
Reversed Four
A personal sense of value is not equated by possessions and social standing.

5 Upright Four
Financial reward for sustained effort.
Reversed Four
Concentrating solely on financial concerns can stifle inner emotions.

6 Upright Four
The tendency to extravagance may limit financial success.
Reversed Four
Suspense or delay causes financial problems.

7 Upright Four
Material wealth does not automatically ensure inner security and well-being.
Reversed Four
Loss of funds causes anxiety.

8 Upright Four
A financial triumph results in sense of emptiness and dissatisfaction.
Reversed Four
The stagnation of creative energy often blocks spiritual and material progress.

9 Upright Four
A gift or an inheritance.
Reversed Four
Miserly tendencies caused by fear of loss.

10 Upright Four
Leadership, power, and material wealth.
Reversed Four
Financial problems through spending unwisely.

5 Possible goal or destiny

10 The final outcome

1

2 Immediate influences

Present position of querent

4 Past influences

6 Future influences

9 Querent's hopes and ideals

8 Family and friends

3 Recent influences

7 Querent's negative feelings

Three of PENTACLES

This is the card of recognition in career or work, suggesting training and professionalism, successful business or commercial expansion, monetary reward, and artistic ability that brings renown When reversed, it can mean lack of direction and ignorance.

SUGGESTED READING

1 Upright or Reversed Three
Consistent effort, ability, and professionalism bring fulfillment and success.

2 Upright or Reversed Three
Creative, business, or commercial expansion.

3 Upright Three
Learning to utilize own abilities to the full.
Reversed Three
Haphazard method and lack of direction leads to failure.

4 Upright Three
A growing confidence in own abilities.
Reversed Three
Little progress due to lack. of motivation and direction.

5 Upright Three
An initial success, which if followed up, leads to improved status and gain.
Reversed Three
More hard work is needed before standard is reached.

6 Upright Three
An inner satisfaction from work well done.
Reversed Three
Disorganization of business and financial matters.

7 Upright Three
Self-honesty and the desire to develop abilities bring a decision.
Reversed Three
More training or education is needed before success can be attained.

8 Upright Three
Cooperation from friends, a society, or a group.
Reversed Three
Ignorance and selfishness spell failure.

9 Upright Three
The development of great talent and ability.
Reversed Three
Conceit in own ability often prevents additional learning.

10 Upright Three
Esteem and honor gained through use of talents.
Reversed Three
The preoccupation with commercial and financial gain results in mediocrity.

5 Possible goal or destiny		10 The final outcome

	1			9 Querent's hopes and ideals
4 Past influences	2 Immediate influences		6 Future influences	8 Family and friends
	Present position of querent			7 Querent's negative feelings
	3 Recent influences			

123

TWO of PENTACLES

Balance amid change is the theme of this card. It can signify news concerning a journey or change of abode, the use of one talent to succeed, and literary ability. When reversed, it can mean emotional instability that could cause delays, or difficulty in launching a new project.

SUGGESTED READING

1 Upright or Reversed Two
Harmony achieved in the midst of change.

2 Upright or Reversed Two
Reassuring news or joyful communication which brings a change for the better.

3 Upright Two
Difficulty in starting something new.
Reversed Two
Fluctuation in fortunes causes a delay.

4 Upright Two
The abillty to manage two situations sucessfully at the same time.
Reversed Two
Care needed in organizing time and energy.

5 Upright Two
Success in one direction.
Reversed Two
The choice of direction is crucial to future success.

6 Upright Two
The use of one talent to achieve success.
Reversed Two
Difficulty and delay in starting something new.

7 Upright Two
News pertaining to change of residence or a forthcoming journey.
Reversed Two
Inability to handle more than one issue at a time.

8 Upright Two
A generous gift or help from others.
Reversed Two
Hostile influences will try to deflect purpose.

9 Upright Two
Stamina, skill, and talent combine to bring reward.
Reversed Two
Control of fluctuating moods necessary for success.

10 Upright Two
New move brings joy and gain.
Reversed Two
Skillful manipulation and persistence needed to achieve one's goal.

5 Possible goal or destiny		10 The final outcome
1		9 Querent's hopes and ideals
4 Past influences	2 Immediate influences / Present position of querent	6 Future influences
		8 Family and friends
3 Recent influences		7 Querent's negative feelings

Ace of Pentacles

Stoicism and materialism are expressed by this card. It can mean the start of a profitable enterprise, love of the physical side of life, and pride in worldly achievement. When reversed, it can denote overconfidence, greed, and wealth without happiness due to spiritual poverty.

SUGGESTED READING

1 Upright or Reversed Ace
Inner and outer riches; material success.

2 Upright or Reversed Ace
Future security based on a firm foundation.

3 Upright Ace
The means available for material achievement.
Reversed Ace
Stability and stamina needed to see something through.

4 Upright Ace
The beginning of an enterprise which brings financial reward.
Reversed Ace
Follow inner voice to ensure the right choice is made.

5 Upright Ace
Wealth, and material and physical comfort.
Reversed Ace
The fear of taking a risk can prevent progress.

6 Upright Ace
An unexpected gift; a win or a small legacy which helps put plans into action.
Reversed Ace
Avoid overconfidence. Check plans carefully.

7 Upright Ace
Persistence needed to utilize resources.
Reversed Ace
Greed results in spiritual poverty and dissatisfaction.

8 Upright Ace
The arrival of an important letter or some reassuring news.
Reversed Ace
Too great an appreciation of physical beauty could mislead or entrap.

9 Upright Ace
Happiness and prosperity reign.
Reversed Ace
Prosperity without happiness.

10 Upright Ace
Spiritual blessing and material success.
Reversed Ace
Wealth wasted or misused.

	5 Possible goal or destiny		**10** The final outcome
	1		**9** Querent's hopes and ideals
4 Past influences	**2** Immediate influences / Present position of querent	**6** Future influences	**8** Family and friends
	3 Recent influences		**7** Querent's negative feelings

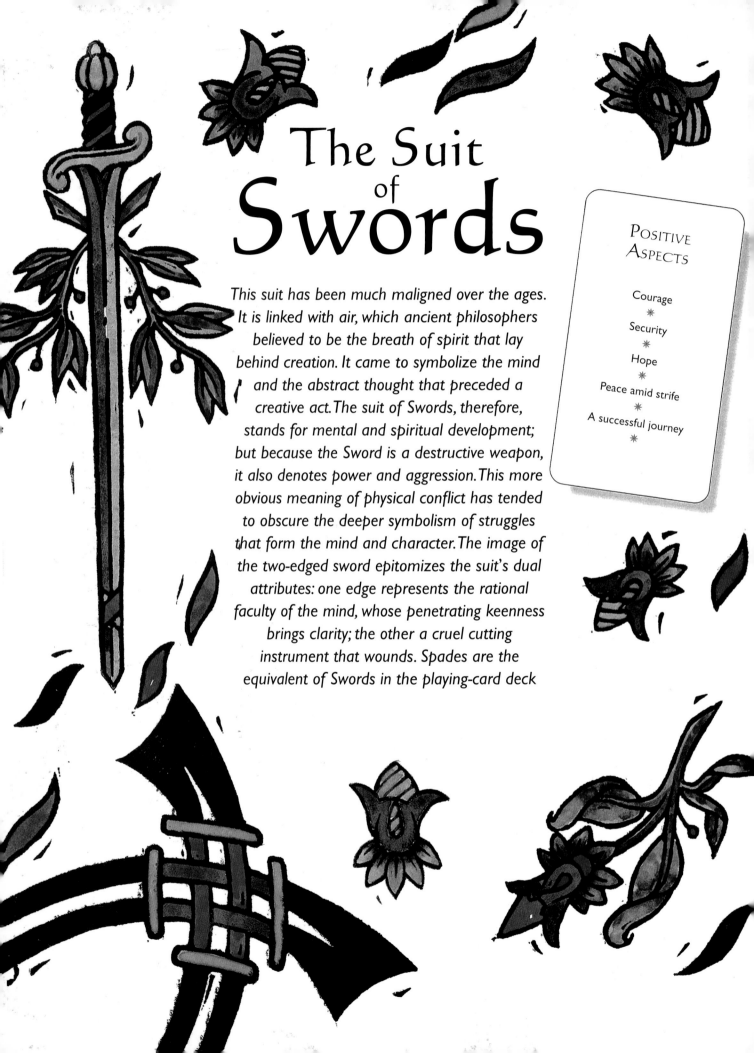

The Suit of Swords

This suit has been much maligned over the ages. It is linked with air, which ancient philosophers believed to be the breath of spirit that lay behind creation. It came to symbolize the mind and the abstract thought that preceded a creative act. The suit of Swords, therefore, stands for mental and spiritual development; but because the Sword is a destructive weapon, it also denotes power and aggression. This more obvious meaning of physical conflict has tended to obscure the deeper symbolism of struggles that form the mind and character. The image of the two-edged sword epitomizes the suit's dual attributes: one edge represents the rational faculty of the mind, whose penetrating keenness brings clarity; the other a cruel cutting instrument that wounds. Spades are the equivalent of Swords in the playing-card deck

POSITIVE ASPECTS

Courage

✳

Security

✳

Hope

✳

Peace amid strife

✳

A successful journey

✳

NEGATIVE
ASPECTS

Spiritual suffering
*
Loneliness
*
Sacrifice
*
Loss
*
Defeat
*

King of Swords

ROY · D'ÉPÉE

A professional man over 35 with an innovative mind, or an intellectual with strong moral convictions, the King of Swords could be a soldier, lawyer, or government official. He can be cruel, violent, vengeful, and a severe critic. This card also signifies a foreign man or country.

SUGGESTED READING

I **Upright or Reversed King**
A powerful man can help the querent to overcome destructive people or own destructive instincts. Can also mean legal action.

2 **Upright or Reversed King**
The desire to put inspired ideas into practice, possibly with help of an authoritative man, or in a foreign country.

3 **Upright King**
The querent possesses strong intellect and ideas.
Reversed King
Learn that there are other sides to an argument, apart from one's own.

4 **Upright King**
Foresight and strategy will be required to put plans into action.
Reversed King
A tendency to be too critical of those who do not possess strength or high intelligence.

5 **Upright King**
Original ideas bring success and reward.
Reversed King
A legal tangle will take time to unravel.

6 **Upright King**
Guile is needed to deal with destructive opposition.
Reversed King
Anger clouds judgment. Be diplomatic with opposition.

7 **Upright King**
Forgiveness without compassion is sterile.
Reversed King
A detached viewpoint can sometimes stifle emotions.

8 **Upright King**
A victory or triumph over those who delight in destructive gossip.
Reversed King
A foreign man or commercial concern is of great benefit to future plans.

9 **Upright King**
Excellent advice from powerful man gives impetus to plans.
Reversed King
Help given by powerful person will negate another's malicious plans or actions.

IO **Upright King**
Organization and leadership bring fulfillment.
Reversed King
A lack of empathy with others results in sense of isolation.

5 Possible goal or destiny		10 The final outcome
	I	
4 Past influences	2 Immediate influences / Present position of querent	6 Future influences
		9 Querent's hopes and ideals
		8 Family and friends
3 Recent influences		7 Querent's negative feelings

Queen of SWORDS

The widow's card, this carries the connotation of sadness. The Queen of Swords is cautious, strong, and intelligent, but can also be intolerant and spiteful. This card also signifies the conflict between spiritual and material values, and can symbolize a foreign woman or country.

SUGGESTED READING

1 Upright or Reversed Queen
A clever, slightly detached, sometimes sad woman can give sound advice to the querent. Could also mean that struggle brings triumph of the spirit over the material; or a foreign country.

2 Upright or Reversed Queen
A strong woman offers valuable help and counsel.

3 Upright Queen
The ideal of perfection, carried to extremes, can cause loss and pain.
Reversed Queen
A lack of love in the past has left a scar.

4 Upright Queen
Demanding the impossible in a relationship results in loneliness.
Reversed Queen
Unrealistic expectations have created a feeling of inadequacy.

5 Upright Queen
Old beliefs are discarded and a new life beckons.
Reversed Queen
Have faith, be positive; things are improving slowly.

6 Upright Queen
Over-attention to detail can result in failure to view whole picture objectively.
Reversed Queen
Difficulty with finances.

7 Upright Queen
An unconscious striving to prove one's worth comes from past rejection.
Reversed Queen
The old mask is being discarded and brings a new attitude to life.

8 Upright Queen
Allow friends to give; do not be too independent.
Reversed Queen
Wanting one's own way too often ruins friendship.

9 Upright Queen
Happiness comes with the courage to give oneself to others.
Reversed Queen
Malicious gossip can stem from the urge to destroy another's self-sufficiency.

10 Upright Queen
The spirit triumphs over loss and deprivation.
Reversed Queen
The realization that no one is perfect brings inner peace.

	5 Possible goal or destiny		10 The final outcome
	1		9 Querent's hopes and ideals
4 Past influences	2 Immediate influences / Present position of querent	6 Future influences	8 Family and friends
	3 Recent influences		7 Querent's negative feelings

129

Knight of SWORDS

CAVALIER · D'EPEE

A courageous man, over 21 and under 35, who is career-minded, passionate, and ruthless, the Knight of Swords shines in a difficult situation. This card can denote a foreigner, a foreign country, or an imminent conflict; and when nearby cards indicate illness, a surgeon.

SUGGESTED READING

1 Upright or Reversed Knight
A strong, confident young man can help in a future struggle for prestige. A sudden change, a foreign element, the beginning and end of a difficulty.

2 Upright or Reversed Knight
An impetuous young man lends aid to querent, or a foreigner brings help.

3 Upright Knight
The desire for change is very strong.
Reversed Knight
Someone strongly opposes thought of change.

4 Upright Knight
At present be content with planning but not discussing future objectives.
Reversed Knight
It is not yet time to start something new.

5 Upright Knight
An exhilarating prospect of new heights to conquer.
Reversed Knight
Egotistical self-interest can lead to loss of loving friend.

6 Upright Knight
Encouragement and help given by a friend in a career move.
Reversed Knight
A difficult waiting period which teaches tolerance.

7 Upright Knight
A desire to alter circumstances too quickly may damage a relationship.
Reversed Knight
Wait a little longer before going ahead with a new plan.

8 Upright Knight
Help from friend ensures the end of a problem.
Reversed Knight
An insensitive young man may create discord among friends.

9 Upright Knight
New ambitions open up a new vista.
Reversed Knight
Patience is required to solve a long-standing problem.

10 Upright Knight
A sudden change of perspective points to a new direction in life.
Reversed Knight
The needs of others must be considered when making an important decision.

5 Possible goal or destiny		10 The final outcome
	1	9 Querent's hopes and ideals
4 Past influences	2 Immediate influences / Present position of querent / 6 Future influences	8 Family and friends
	3 Recent influences	7 Querent's negative feelings

Knave of Swords

A young person of either sex with an independent turn of mind, who is open to novelty, the Knave of Swords has a childlike curiosity. He or she can be unpredictable, mischievous, frivolous, and cruel to others, yet also diplomatic, or manipulative and devious.

SUGGESTED READING

1 Upright or Reversed Knave
A messenger, news, inner conflict, a business rival, or a foreign person or country.

2 Upright or Reversed Knave
A message bringing unexpected news.

3 Upright Knave
Dormant mental faculties now being stirred into activity.
Reversed Knave
Inner conflict resulting from past injustices.

4 Upright Knave
A strong need to cut through entanglements.
Reversed Knave
Past injuries, if not forgiven, are difficult to forget.

5 Upright Knave
Access to information results in a surge of creativity.
Reversed Knave
The ability to discern the true nature of things is satisfying.

6 Upright Knave
Irritability stems from the desire for change.
Reversed Knave
Skillful negotiation on behalf of others earns praise.

7 Upright Knave
Intuitive feelings should never be ignored.
Reversed Knave
A rival is defeated by playing on his hidden weaknesses.

8 Upright Knave
Grace and dexterity allied to talent bring a feeling of fulfillment.
Reversed Knave
A young person's conduct is both unexpected and unpredictable.

9 Upright Knave
Be prepared for unforeseen opportunity for new creative work.
Reversed Knave
Someone known to you in work or career is considering a new plan or idea of great benefit.

10 Upright Knave
True independence of mind achieved through the ability to perceive clearly.
Reversed Knave
The opinion of others must be evaluated dispassionately before discarding completely.

VALET·D'EPEE

5 Possible goal or destiny

10 The final outcome

1 Immediate influences

2 Immediate influences / Present position of querent

4 Past influences

6 Future influences

9 Querent's hopes and ideals

8 Family and friends

3 Recent influences

7 Querent's negative feelings

Ten of SWORDS

This card can mean the lowest point in a nation's economy or in human affairs. Self-honesty shatters a dream but brings clarity. When reversed, it can mean the end of spiritual darkness, self-acceptance that brings the courage to rise again, and the end of a painful period.

SUGGESTED READING

1 Upright or Reversed Ten
The end of a personal illusion, or a national depression.

2 Upright or Reversed Ten
A lesson to be learned.

3 Upright Ten
Learn to look at the true facts and accept the reality.
Reversed Ten
Anger can be self-destructive. Forgive yourself and others.

4 Upright Ten
A sudden misfortune caused by loss of money or loss of work.
Reversed Ten
Negative thinking will not help in a crisis.

5 Upright Ten
Self-honesty gives the strength to face a situation.
Reversed Ten
A slow improvement in business or health.

6 Upright Eight
Adopting the methods and ideas of others can lead to financial ruin.
Reversed Ten
Past generosity brings unexpected reward.

7 Upright Ten
A deep, inner sense of loss brings the need for spiritual help.
Reversed Ten
A sudden collapse of plans is hard to accept.

8 Upright Ten
The slowing down of financial affairs has an important effect on daily life.
Reversed Ten
New and positive vibrations are on the way.

9 Upright Ten
The aftermath of deep emotional wound results in anger and negative thinking.
Reversed Ten
Self-acceptance results in forgiveness of others.

10 Upright Ten
Take off the rose-colored spectacles and see things as they really are.
Reversed Ten
The lowest point has been reached and it is time to rise up once again.

5 Possible goal or destiny		**10** The final outcome
1 / **2** Immediate influences / Present position of querent		**9** Querent's hopes and ideals
4 Past influences	**6** Future influences	**8** Family and friends
3 Recent influences		**7** Querent's negative feelings

Nine of SWORDS

Self-punishment is the keynote of this card. It can signify an over-attachment to the past, a sense of hopelessness, a period of illness or isolation, and lack of help from others. Reversed meanings are positive: past influences are shed; new productive activity begins; time heals.

SUGGESTED READING

1 Upright or Reversed Nine
Strength and new life as a result of suffering.

2 Upright or Reversed Nine
A burden will soon be lifted.

3 Upright Nine
Repressing productive energy brings a feeling of unfulfillment and unhappiness.
Reversed Nine
Hurt and disappointment caused by others.

4 Upright Nine
Too influenced by the past to enjoy the present.
Reversed Nine
Patience and unselfishness will soon be rewarded.

5 Upright Nine
Freedom comes with the realization that past guilt fuels present misery.
Reversed Nine
Tomorrow brings a feeling of new hope and promise.

6 Upright Nine
Self-accusation results in a feeling of hopelessness.
Reversed Nine
Recognition that harsh standards imposed by others have caused dissatisfaction.

7 Upright Nine
A period of needless anxiety about the future.
Reversed Nine
Have faith; a better time is close on the horizon.

8 Upright Seven
Suffering borne with fortitude and patience is rewarded with love.
Reversed Nine
The necessity to part from loved ones and travel to a new environment.

9 Upright Nine
A difficult choice to be made, entailing sacrifice.
Reversed Nine
The commencement of new productive activity.

10 Upright Nine
A burden accepted with passive obedience will become a blessing.
Reversed Nine
Tume heals all wounds.

	5 Possible goal or destiny	**10** The final outcome
	1 / **2** Immediate influences / Present position of querent	**9** Querent's hopes and ideals
4 Past influences	**6** Future influences	**8** Family and friends
	3 Recent influences	**7** Querent's negative feelings

133

Eight of SWORDS

This card indicates that patience, self-confidence, and self-honesty are needed. Indecision arises from fear of confrontation, blindness, or duplicity. When reversed, it can mean that progress will soon begin: negative feelings will fade, hurts heal, and self-confidence return.

SUGGESTED READING

1 Upright or Reversed Eight
A cycle of misfortune comes to an end.

2 Upright or Reversed Eight
Courage and patience overcome adversity and feelings of restriction.

3 Upright Eight
Fear of confrontation comes from reluctance to hurt others.
Reversed Eight
Kindness is sometimes regarded as weakness by those who manipulate.

4 Upright Eight
Inability to act because of concern for others.
Reversed Eight
Temporary sickness as a result of stress.

5 Upright Eight
Faith in oneself is regained after acknowledging own past mistakes.
Reversed Eight
Impulsive generosity will be repaid a hundredfold.

6 Upright Eight
Lack of self-confidence prevents taking chances.
Reversed Eight
A sign will show which path to take for future happiness.

7 Upright Eight
Fear of failure prevents attempting something new.
Reversed Eight
A slow but steady return to health and productivity.

8 Upright Eight
The demands of others bring pain and anxiety.
Reversed Eight
Patience and attention to detail deflect criticism.

9 Upright Eight
Bonds will soon be broken, bringing freedom from restriction.
Reversed Eight
A sense of restriction causes difficulty in making an important decision.

10 Upright Eight
The slow realization that indecision and lack of self-confidence stem from own emotional blindness.
Reversed Eight
Wounds are healed and a positive attitude returns.

5
Possible goal or destiny

10
The final outcome

1

2
Immediate influences

Present position of querent

9
Querent's hopes and ideals

4
Past influences

6
Future influences

8
Family and friends

3
Recent influences

7
Querent's negative feelings

Seven of Swords

This card emphasizes the need for diplomacy to attain an objective; aggressive tactics would be disastrous. It also suggests that greed may cause unprincipled behavior. When reversed, it can mean that plans go awry and dwelling on mistakes prohibits progress.

SUGGESTED READING

1 Upright or Reversed Seven
The use of brain not brawn achieves an objective.

2 Upright or Reversed Seven
Guile and diplomacy are both required for facing a difficult situation successfully.

3 Upright Seven
A new project is considered while an older one waits on the sidelines.
Reversed Seven
Dwelling on past mistakes can prevent making progress in a new project.

4 Upright Seven
Things not working out the way they were planned.
Reversed Seven
Failure of nerve could mean the collapse of a daring idea or adventurous plan.

5 Upright Seven
Prudence and foresight defeat all opposition.
Reversed Seven
Victory is almost won. Do not surrender too soon.

6 Upright Seven
Guile and strategy, plus a knowledge of others' weaknesses, will help to defeat opposition.
Reversed Seven
Hypocrisy can leave a bad taste in the mouth.

7 Upright Seven
Have alternative plan ready in case of emergency.
Reversed Seven
Something valuable comes back to you unexpectedly.

8 Upright Seven
A possibility of slight injury from sporting activity.
Reversed Seven
Make sure you are claiming what is your own by right.

9 Upright Seven
False pride could prevent taking genuine help and advice from others.
Reversed Seven
Overconfidence can sometimes lead to loss.

10 Upright Seven
Direct confrontation with others is disastrous.
Reversed Seven
Courage, perseverance, and foresight result in triumph.

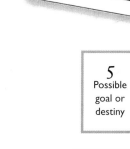

	5 Possible goal or destiny		10 The final outcome
4 Past influences	I, 2 Immediate influences, Present position of querent	6 Future influences	9 Querent's hopes and ideals
	3 Recent influences		8 Family and friends
			7 Querent's negative feelings

135

Six of SWORDS

The card of travel to a more pleasing destination, or an overseas visitor who brings good news, the Six of Swords can also mean the end of a difficult cycle, a risk that results in gain, or a leap in self-understanding. When reversed, there is no immediate solution, so be patient.

SUGGESTED READING

1 Upright or Reversed Six
The solving of immediate problems or success after a period of anxiety.

2 Upright or Reversed Six
A change of position or environment brings fulfillment.

3 Upright Six
A major hurdle has been passed without loss of dignity or self-respect.
Reversed Six
Frustration in career brings a strong desire for change.

4 Upright Six
Great understanding and objectivity have been developed as a result of past trials and tribulations.
Reversed Six
Spiritual guidance is needed to surmount present constricting circumstances.

5 Upright Six
A stressful period is ended and progress resumed.
Reversed Six
Obstacles which appear will not prevent progress.

6 Upright Six
Peace of mind after prolonged worry and anxiety.
Reversed Six
Do not be afraid of taking risks if matters have been carefully considered.

7 Upright Six
Advent of a new friend or a visitor from overseas.
Reversed Six
A relationship will be severed through a move or journey.

8 Upright Six
A move to a better, happier environment.
Reversed Six
A move or journey will be temporarily postponed.

9 Upright Six
Mental ability and insight combine to reach a higher level of consciousness.
Reversed Six
There is no way out at present, but help will come.

10 Upright Six
Effort and fortitude are still required to ensure permanent gain.
Reversed Six
Evading or escaping from problems will only postpone the inevitable moment.

5 Possible goal or destiny		10 The final outcome
	1	
4 Past influences	2 Immediate influences / Present position of querent	6 Future influences
		9 Querent's hopes and ideals
		8 Family and friends
3 Recent influences		7 Querent's negative feelings

Five of Swords

This card signifies the need to acknowledge one's limitations, accept defeat, and swallow false pride in order to proceed. It can denote unfairness, slander, cowardice, or a lack of sensitivity. When reversed, a triumph turns to humiliation, or fear of defeat brings loss.

SUGGESTED READING

1 Upright or Reversed Five
The necessity to face the cause of failure before new success is achieved.

2 Upright or Reversed Five
Accepting own limitations leads to future triumph.

3 Upright Five
Overestimating own capabilities results in failure.
Reversed Five
A business failure will slowly be resolved.

4 Upright Five
An unrealistic attitude to finances causes loss.
Reversed Five
Self-gain and self-interest can repel friendship.

5 Upright Five
Defeat faced realistically promises future triumph.
Reversed Five
Thoughtlessness can cause an unhappy separation.

6 Upright Five
The need to build a secure financial foundation.
Reversed Five
A narrow escape from financial ruin.

7 Upright Five
A possibility of loss through unfair, or perhaps illegal, practices.
Reversed Five
Intrigue and deception caused by untrustworthy associate.

8 Upright Five
Misreading a sensitive situation results in a difficult emotional problem.
Reversed Five
A sudden separation from a partner or close friend.

9 Upright Five
The use of force can result in temporary triumph and lasting humiliation.
Reversed Five
Diplomacy not belligerence will win the day.

10 Upright Five
Failure in one direction leads to triumph in another area.
Reversed Five
Learning to swallow pride and assess own abilities honestly brings peace.

5 Possible goal or destiny		10 The final outcome
4 Past influences	1 / 2 Immediate influences / Present position of querent	6 Future influences
	3 Recent influences	

9 Querent's hopes and ideals

8 Family and friends

7 Querent's negative feelings

Four of Swords

Peace after pain is the theme of this card, which suggests rest, meditation, or a period of convalescence after anxiety or illness. When reversed, it denotes a feeling of isolation; the postponement of a decision that must be made; and the need to be wise and diplomatic.

SUGGESTED READING

1 Upright or Reversed Four
Peace and order come out of struggle and strife.

2 Upright or Reversed Four
Quiet needed to examine thoughts and organize life.

3 Upright Four
Becoming prepared for change by making plans.
Reversed Four
A temporary feeling of being out of touch with life.

4 Upright Four
A shadow is moving gradually away from your sun.
Reversed Four
Problems in work must be dealt with diplomatically.

5 Upright Four
A major decision must be taken, not postponed.
Reversed Four
Avoiding positive action simply delays the inevitable.

6 Upright Four
Avoid hasty decisions; take time to discover what is going to be best for you.
Reversed Four
Recuperation after an illness or period of low energy.

7 Upright Four
A time to renew energies after an episode of stress.
Reversed Four
A renewal of faith brings new hope and energy.

8 Upright Four
The discovery of strength in reserve brings a new feeling of self-respect.
Reversed Four
Refusal to face opposition only delays the dreaded moment.

9 Upright Four
Wait with patience; things are now changing for the better.
Reversed Four
Avoid making rash promises. Things are changing rapidly.

10 Upright Four
A difficult battle that tested body and spirit has now been won.
Reversed Four
Illness or a period of enforced seclusion proves to be a blessing in disguise.

5 Possible goal or destiny	**10** The final outcome
1 **2** Immediate influences Present position of querent	**9** Querent's hopes and ideals
4 Past influences **6** Future influences	**8** Family and friends
3 Recent influences	**7** Querent's negative feelings

Three of Swords

This card always means upheaval and sorrow, but it has the connotation of clearing the ground for something new. It can denote the breaking of partnerships, but after pain, a healing follows. When reversed, it means dwelling on old hurts, upheaval in the environment, and civil strife.

SUGGESTED READING

1 Upright or Reversed Three
An upheaval prepares the way for something new.

2 Upright or Reversed Three
An emotional upheaval is the prelude to a better future.

3 Upright Three
A difficult emotional period in close relationships.
Reversed Three
Pain caused by separation from family or loved one.

4 Upright Three
The necessary destruction of the outworn or obsolete.
Reversed Three
Quarreling causes divisions in family or partnership.

5 Upright Three
A new future is now on the horizon.
Reversed Three
Blindness in a relationship is suddenly recognized.

6 Upright Three
The ground is being cleared for something new.
Reversed Three
The breaking of a promise brings discord and quarrels.

7 Upright Three
Think before you speak or it could be too late to mend a quarrel.
Reversed Three
Try to be a peacemaker; there are always two sides to every argument.

8 Upright Three
A breakup of a partnership or marriage.
Reversed Three
Sorrow and tears over a faithless lover.

9 Upright Three
Disappointment in emotional affair caused by self-deception.
Reversed Three
Three-sided relationships are seldom resolved amicably.

10 Upright Three
The darkness lessens; dawn is coming.
Reversed Three
Past hurts, unless forgiven, will affect future happiness.

5 Possible goal or destiny		**10** The final outcome
1 **2** Immediate influences Present position of querent	**6** Future influences	**9** Querent's hopes and ideals
4 Past influences		**8** Family and friends
3 Recent Influences		**7** Querent's negative feelings

TWO of SWORDS

The card of stalemate, the Two of Swords can signify good coming out of evil, help in adversity, a difficult choice, or a situation that brings spiritual satisfaction. When reversed, it implies impotence, the need to leave the past behind, and making the wrong choice.

SUGGESTED READING

1 Upright or Reversed Two
A difficult decision needs to be made soon.

2 Upright or Reversed Two
A deadlock in affairs through inability to make a decision.

3 Upright Two
A difficult choice which demands self-honesty.
Reversed Two
An emotional problem causes indecision.

4 Upright Two
The need for a new approach to a problem.
Reversed Two
Impotence through the inability to take action.

5 Upright Two
Equilibrium gained after strife and dissent.
Reversed Two
A need for careful thought before committing self.

6 Upright Two
The refusal to face a situation merely delays necessary disruption.
Reversed Two
An upsetting situation caused by malicious troublemaker.

7 Upright Two
Speaking honestly clears the air and results in love and peace.
Reversed Four
A lack of self-control causes tension in relationships.

8 Upright Two
A lasting friendship made by sharing similar problems.
Reversed Two
Be careful of sharing personal confidences with a new acquaintance.

9 Upright Two
Success will come in one direction.
Reversed Two
Unsure as to which path it would be best to take.

10 Upright Two
A new undertaking brings recognition, success, and reward.
Reversed Two
Affairs are moving fast. Be careful – haste could result in a wrong decision.

5 Possible goal or destiny		**10** The final outcome
1 Immediate influences		**9** Querent's hopes and ideals
4 Past influences	**2** Present position of querent **6** Future influences	**8** Family and friends
3 Recent influences		**7** Querent's negative feelings

Ace of Swords

A card of great force, either for good or ill (depending upon the surrounding cards), the Ace of Swords can mean conquest. It carries a sense of something unpreventable that will change the entire life. When reversed, it implies victory with disastrous results and weakness of will.

SUGGESTED READING

1 Upright or Reversed Ace
An inner and outer change is due to happen.

2 Upright or Reversed Ace
An inevitable event alters entire life.

3 Upright Ace
Brilliant powers of thought and idealism are combined in a just cause.
Reversed Ace
Check details. Make sure future plans are in order.

4 Upright Ace
A progress in affairs which cannot be stopped.
Reversed Ace
Refuse to expect the worst and stay positive.

5 Upright Ace
Just rewards for past efforts are assured.
Reversed Ace
A mental awakening results in shedding of outworn beliefs.

6 Upright Ace
The courage to put creative thought into action.
Reversed Ace
Conflict with others over new ideas or plans.

7 Upright Ace
An inner freedom from restraints imposed in the past.
Reversed Ace
Pressuring others will not achieve anything; success comes in its own time.

8 Upright Ace
Know your true friends by the support they give for a new venture.
Reversed Ace
Opposition from others, but success is inevitable despite this.

9 Upright Ace
The seeds of success germinate swiftly.
Reversed Ace
The emergence of a new creative viewpoint depends on the will to fight.

10 Upright Ace
Success is assured, despite apparently overwhelming odds.
Reversed Ace
Accept help and advice and concentrate on a specific goal.

	5 Possible goal or destiny		**10** The final outcome
4 Past influences	**1** / **2** Immediate influences / Present position of querent	**6** Future influences	**9** Querent's hopes and ideals
			8 Family and friends
	3 Recent influences		**7** Querent's negative feelings

INDEX

Page numbers in *italics* refer to illustrations

CREDITS

Marseilles Deck

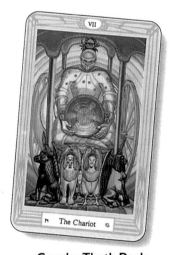

Crowley Thoth Deck

IJJ Swiss Deck

**Pierpont Morgan-Bergamo
Visconti-Sforza Deck**

Ukiyoe Deck

Quarto would like to acknowledge and thank the following for providing pictures used in this book:

Illustrations from the **Marseilles deck** reproduced by kind permission of France Cartes Grimaud, BP 49, 54132 Saint Max Cédex (France). Further reproduction prohibited.

Illustrations from the **Crowley Thoth Tarot** and **IJJ Swiss Tarot Cards** reproduced by permission of AGM AG Muller, CH-8212 Neuhausen, Switzerland. Further reproduction prohibited.
© Crowley: 1944, 1962 OTO International, USA/AGM AGMuller, Switzerland
© IJJ: 1972 AGM AGMuller, Switzerland

Illustrations from the **Pierpont Morgan-Bergamo Visconti-Sforza Tarocchi** and **Ukiyoe Tarot Decks** reproduced by permission of US Games Systems, Inc, Stamford, CT 06902 USA. Copyright © Pierpont Morgan-Bergamo Visconti-Sforza: 1975 and Ukiyoe: 1982 by US Games Systems Inc. Further reproduction prohibited.

Art Resource-Giraudon / Pierpont Morgan Library, New York: pages 8, 9 (below), 10; Giraudon / Musée des Beaux-Art de Rennes: page 9 (above); Giraudon: pages 10, 15; Alinari-Giraudon: pages 14, 16; Christie's Images: page 17.

All other photographs and illustrations are the copyright of Quarto. While every effort has been made to acknowledge copyright holders, we would like to apologize should there have been any omissions.

Quarto would also like to thank David Westnedge for his kind assistance in the making of this book.